RECORD

OF THE

PARISH LIST OF DEATHS.

1785—1819.

BY

REV. WILLIAM BENTLEY, D. D.,

PASTOR OF THE EAST CHURCH, SALEM.

[FROM THE HISTORICAL COLLECTIONS OF THE ESSEX INSTITUTE.]

CLEARFIELD

Originally published
Salem, Massachusetts, 1882

Reprinted for
Clearfield Company, Inc. by
Genealogical Publishing Co., Inc.
Baltimore, Maryland
2002

International Standard Book Number: 0-8063-5171-3

Made in the United States of America

INTRODUCTION.

This Parish List of Deaths, recorded by Rev. William Bentley during his ministry in Salem, has been prepared and edited by Mr. Ira J. Patch, of Salem, the well-known genealogist.

Mr. Bentley was an eminent scholar, a zealous antiquarian, a revered and honored minister, and indefatigably industrious in collecting and recording anything relating to his studies, his pursuits, his parish and his life. He was born in Boston, June 22, 1759; a graduate of Harvard in the class of 1777, and from which he received the honorary degree of D.D., in 1819, ordained over the East church and society in Salem, 1783. Died Dec. 29, 1819.

His great collection of manuscripts have, since his death, been deposited by his executor, in the archives of the American Antiquarian Society.

The printing of them, or a selection of them, carefully edited, would be a valuable contribution to our historical literature.

PARISH LIST OF DEATHS BEGUN 1785.

1. Jan. 9. A child of Master John Watson in childbed.
2. April. 17. Rebecca Bushnel an. æt. 41 of a consumption.
3. April 25. David Newhall an. æt. 45 of a consumption.
4. May 27. Thomas Keene, æt. 10 months, of dropsy in the head.
5. July 11. Mercy, wife of Wm. Browne, an. æt. 50, of apoplexy.
6. July 22. Mary Tozzer, widow, an. æt. 86. Aged.
7. July 30. Samuel, of Joseph & Abigail Lambert, æt. 9 mo. Convulsions.
8. Aug. 1. Stephen, of Elizabeth & John Foster, æt. 15 mo. Fever.
9. Aug. 11. Eunice, wife of Philip English, an. æt. 50. King's Evil.
10. Aug. 13. Sally, of Joseph & Peggy Prat, æt. 12 mo. Fever.
11. Sept. 13. Lydia, d. of Capt. Fiske, 17 years, 6 mo. Consumption.
12. Oct. 2. Peggy, d. of Joseph & Martha Renew, 17 years. Dropsy in head.
13. Oct. 11. Joseph Hodges, an. æt. 70 & 7 mo. Lethargy.

14. Nov. 12. John S., of Wm. & Mehitabel Patterson, 22 mo. Consumption.
15. Nov. 26. Elizabeth Leach in the family of John Watson, an. æt. 21. Dropsy in head.
16. Nov. 30. Patty, wife of John Fiske Esq., an. æt. 32. Consumption.
17. Dec. 10. Ruth Phippen, maiden, an. æt. 66. Aged.
18. Dec. 30. Betsey, d. of Samuel & Elizabeth Masury, an. æt. 2. Consumption.

LIST OF DEATHS FOR 1786.

19. Jan. 19. News of death of Capt. Jacob Clark, æt. 35. Fever. Left a widow & two small children, one male. Died on his passage fr. West Indies.
20. Jan. 26. Mary Carrol, widow, æt. 60. Consumption. Left a daughter married to a Mr. Parrotte.
21. Feb. 18. Hannah Keene, wife of Thomas Keene, æt. 32. Consumption. Formerly Silver, natural daughter of Jona. Cloutman. No children.
22. Feb. 19. John Crowninshield, s. of widow Hannah, æt. 24. Dysentery. Left a widow, d. of Capt. Hawthorne. No children. Taken sick abroad.
23. March 9. John Gunnerson, æt. 64. Palsy. He was of Kittery. Left widow and three married children, one daughter m. Harrington. 4 g. children.
24. March 20. Sarah Cloutman, maiden æt. 28. Consumption. Daughter of Widow Mary Cloutman, who has 3 children; 2 sons left.
25. April 23. Male child of Benj. & Mary Crowninshield, died in 12 hours after delivery. One male child living.
26. April 23. Male child of John & Hannah Patter-

son, died in 13 hours after delivery. Two children living, one male.

27. June 13. Edmund Whittemore, æt. 67. Palsy. Wife dead, has left 11 children, 4 males. 8 married.

28. June 24. Female child of Elisha & Mary Gunnison, still born. The first child.

29. June 25. Capt. Richard Masury, returned home from sea, æt. 58. Died in the road to his house of a fever. Has left a wife, 3 sons & 2 daughters; a daughter married.

30. July 7. Anna, child of Daniel & Mary Cloutman, æt. 25 days. Convulsions attending the chin cough.

31. July 23. Sarah Masury, wife of Richard Masury, æt. 56. Consumption, about a month after her husband.

32. July 30. Samuel, son of John & Susannah Gunnerson, æt. 10 mos. Fever attending the chin cough.

33. Aug. 1. Capt. Ebenezer Peirce, fever, æt. 43, on his passage from the West Indies. Left a wife and one married daughter, two small children, one male.

34. Aug. 6. Benjamin Gale, æt. 24. Consumption. He has left a wife and one male child. Returned from sea sick.

35. Aug. 28. Thomas Hutcheson, æt. 46. Fever. He has left a wife and seven children; one daughter married to a Ropes.

36. Sept. 1. Sarah, dau. of Benj. & Susanna Dean, æt. 13 mos. Convulsions after a languishment attend'g the chin cough.

37. Sept. 27. Martha, wife of Caleb Bangs, æt. 26. Consumption. Has left a husband and one child, christened Thomas.

38. Oct. 3. Anna, wife of Penn Townsend, æt. 53. Consumption, lingering sickness. Left a husband and two daughters, one married.

39. Oct. 24. A female, natural daughter of Louis Cox, æt. 14 mos. Vomiting and purging.

40. Oct. 25. John Locke, son of Hunlock & Sarah Palfrey, æt. 18 mos. Water in the head. Four children left, one male.

41. Oct. 28. Edward, son of Benj. & Margaret Nourse, æt. 11 mos. Bloody flux. They have 3 children, two males.

42. Nov. 29. William Chever, æt. 35. Fever. He has left a second wife and 3 children, 2 males.

43. Dec. 29. News of the death of Capt. Adam Welman. Fever, æt. 42. He has left a large family, three classes of children: his wife's by a former husband, his own by a former wife, his own by the present wife, 9 in number; a very aged father and a brother to his present wife, a non compos. Welman, Pierce and Clark died in the same vessel in the course of this year, as the times show.

LIST OF DEATHS FOR 1787.

44. Feb. 5. Timothy Welman, æt. 91, of old age. He has left one dau., 27 grandchildren and 21 great grandchildren.

45. Feb. 6. Ann Willis, in the Almshouse for many years, æt. 89, of old age. She had been married and has left two children, a son in the Almshouse.

46. Feb. 24. William Clark, æt. 30. Epilepsy. Son of Widow Margaret. He had been troubled with the fits above 15 years and was deprived of reason.

47. Mar. 7. A male child of Rebecca, wife of William Chever, late deceased, within 24 hours after delivery.

48. Mar. 30. John Brown, carpenter, æt. 83. Old age. He has left five married children, a son John and Mrs. Moses, Coombs, Cooke and Nourse.

49. Apr. 6. Mary, wife of Benj. Gardner, æt. 56. Consumption. She was named Briers; her parents are living in Marblehead; former husbands were Ferguson and Basset (living two daughters by the first).

50. Apr. 24. John Brown, a Swede, æt. 18, at Capt. Moses Townsend's. Consumption. He was brought by the Capt. from Trinidad, a stranger.

51. May 6. News of William Masury, æt. 18, on April 19th. He was drowned at sea, off the Carolinas, from on board Capt. Roach.

52. May 20. Edward, natural son of Abigail Masury, 20 months old. He fell from the stairs and injured the brain; expired in 40 hours.

53. June 18. Daniel Silver, son of Francis & Hannah, æt. 17 years. Fever. He died upon his return from sea in Capt. Sleuman. Only a mother-in-law living.

54. July 4. Benjamin Archer, æt. 37. Fever, non compos. He died in the work house. He has a brother Jona. and two sisters living.

55. Hannah, d. of Richard Gales & Hannah Pearson. Fever, æt. 14 months. One child, a boy, still in the family. *He* from Whitehaven.

56. Aug. 27. News of the death of Capt. Nathan Brown, æt. 45. He has left a second wife and three children; two sons and a daughter, one son by the first wife. He died of a fever at Martinico, Aug. 7, 1787.

57. Sept. 5. Thomas, s. of Jonathan & Elizabeth Mason, 18 months. He died of vomiting and purging after long illness.

58. Sept. 15. Joshua Richardson, s. of Joshua & Eunice Leavitt, 14 months. The only child, died of consumption.

59. Sept. 23. News of the death of Capt. Richard Hodges, æt. 25, died Aug. 17, of fever, in Demerari. He has left a wife and one child, female.

60. Sept. 28. Hannah, wife of Nathaniel Knowlton, æt. 23. Childbed. She was a Fitz of Ipswich and sister-in-law to her husband. Fœtus dead.

61. Oct. 6. Peter, s. of Samuel & Elizabeth Murray, 16 months. He died of a fever, and was the youngest of 6 children.

62. Nov. 1. Sally, d. of Edward & Peggy Allen, æt. 7 years. Died of the throat distemper, after 20 days.

63. Nov. 3. Elizabeth, wife of Nathaniel Eastey, æt. 43. Atrophy. She had been delirious for six months; has left six children, 2 males, a daughter married.

64. Nov. 9. Thomas Elkins, æt. 17, was drowned on his passage from Madeira homewards. My landlady has two children left.

65. Nov. 22. John Gardner, s. of Abijah & Mary Hitchins, æt. 2 years and 2 months. Throat distemper.

66. Dec. 8. Elizabeth Marsh, æt. 37. Consumption. Her husband, John Marsh, long absent. Five children, three males.

67. Dec. 14. Mary, w. of Rev'd James Diman, æt. 65. Swoon, died very suddenly. She has left 5 children, 2 sons.

LIST OF DEATHS FOR 1788.

68. Feb. 9. Samuel Preston, æt. 21. Consumption. Son of Andrew Preston, who has 6 children, 3 males. Taken sick abroad.

69. Mar. 24. Joseph King, æt. 28. Consumption. He has left a wife and three female children, she in childbed and very poor.

70. June 20. William C., s. of Benj. & Susannah Dean, æt. 13 months. Perished in a vault into which it fell from the neglect of the children to whom it was entrusted.

71. July 1. Samuel Murray, æt. 57, after long confinement. He has left a wife and three children, one son.

72. July 17. Pickering, s. of John & Elizabeth Andrew, æt. a month. Suddenly, after violent crying. They have a numerous family.

73. Aug. 8. Hannah Murray, widow of Jonathan, æt. 55, from long disorders in the stomach. She has left an only daughter.

74. Sept. 2. Benjamin W., s. of Thomas & Lydia Dean, æt. 2. The middle child of three christened Sept. 30, 1787.

75. Sept. 6. Jonathan, s. of Jonathan & Susannah Newhall, æt. 21 months. Vomiting and purging. This Newhall lately from Lynn.

76. Oct. 1. Paul Mansfield, æt. 27, in the workhouse.

77. Oct. 8. Reverend James Diman, æt. 81. Age. He has left two sons and three daughters.

78. Oct. 12. Martha Ward, widow of John, æt. 75. Aged. Buried by Col. Pickman from widow Webb's. Died in the Almshouse.

79. Nov. 4. News of Richard Masury, æt. 25, drowned from on board Capt. Allen, outward bound.

80. Dec. 6. Betsey, d. of Nathaniel & Eunice Richardson, aged 11 months, weak from its birth.

LIST OF DEATHS FOR 1789.

81. Jan. 7. Rachel, wife of Ebenezer Ward, æt. 72. Atrophy sen. Left a husband, two sons and two daughters.

82. May 8. A female negro child of Primus & Violet Grant, æt. 7 days. The first a native of Africa, the second of Woburn, Middlesex.

83. May 12. News of Edmund Kimball, æt. 37. Drowned March 28 in the West Indies from on board Capt. Jo. Lambert. He has left a wife and 4 children, 3 sons.

84. May. News of Capt. William Fairfield, æt. 41. Shot by the slaves in their generous attempt to recover their liberty on March 26.

85. July. News of the death of George Waters, æt. 24. Shot by the guards in the Verd Islands on 13th May.

86. July 14. Margaret, wife of Joseph Searle, æt. 71. Gravel. Married at 60 years of age. She was a Becket.

87. Sept. 11. Sarah, d. of Joseph & Mary Waters, æt. 8 months. Atrophy infantile. They have three daughters left.

88. Sept. News of Benj. Hill. He was drowned from the vessel July 1, Capt. H. White, Commander, æt. 29. He has left a widow and two children, she with child.

89. Sept. 21. John, son of James & Elizabeth Archer, æt. 10 months, æt. 27. They have one male child left.

90. ———. Mary, g. d. of Mary Knap, widow, æt. 16 months. Worms. The mother was engaged to a young man who was drowned at sea.

91. Oct. 5. Female child of Nathaniel & Sarah Silsbee, æt. 13 days. Humour in mouth. They have four children, 3 males.

92. Oct. 7. Elizabeth, d. of Benjamin & Elizabeth Brown, æt. 16 months. It was their only child.

93. Oct. 28. Andrew, s. of Thomas & Elizabeth Chipman, æt. 18 months. They have three children, all sons.

94. Dec. 1. John Ward, æt. 52, of lingering sick-

ness. He has left a second wife. His own children by a former wife are 4 sons and 2 daughters.

95. Dec. 6. Elisha Gunnison, æt. 33. Consumption, attending W. India Flux. He has left a wife with child.

LIST OF DEATHS FOR 1790.

96. Jan. 17. Marshall Stocker, æt. 39 years. His sickness was the West India disorder. He has left a wife and one child.

97. Jan. 20. Rebecca Ashby, æt. 19 years. Consumption. She was a Hill. Has left a husband, but no children.

98. Jan. 23. Elizabeth, wife of John Bechet, æt. 44, suddenly. She has left five of her own children, two sons, survivors. See No. 16.

99. Feb. 9. Mary, wife of David Hilliard, æt. 71. Age. She has left three daughters, two married and one a widow.

100. Feb. 28. Rufus, s. of Ebenezer Phippen, æt. 5. Worms.

101. Mar. 2. Harry, s. of Ebenezer Phippen, æt. 18 mos. Consumption.

These two children of the same parents. Six left, three sons, etc.

102. Mar. 16. Thomas Stevens, æt. 27. Drowned. He was captain of the Sch. Abigail, which was shipwrecked on the Londoner Rock off Thatcher's Island, Cape Ann. He has left a wife and two children, she near delivery.

103. Mar. 16. Sam'l Wellman, æt. 22. Mate in the Abigail and brother-in-law to the Capt.

104. Mar. 21. Mary Cloutman, æt. 66. Consumption. She was at Webb. Has left 4 children, 2 daughters unmarried, 2 sons married.

105. Apr. 30. Female child of Mary Cloutman, æt. 8 months. Natural child. Atrophia infantilis.
106. May 17. Thomas, son of Thomas & Elizabeth Parsons, æt. 6 years. After the measles in consumption.
107. June 1. Stephen Clark, s. of Widow Margaret C., æt. 25. He died of the small pox, which he took at Charleston, S. C. Died at the Hospital.
108. June 5. Sarah Dighton, wife of Richard D., æt. 34. No children. See Day Book.
109. June 13. Mary Collins, widow, æt. 78, under long infirmity. She has left a son and daughter with families.
110. June 24. Ruth Webb, wife of Micah Webb, æt. 22. She was a Putnam and died of a consumption, much lamented.
111. July 6. Abraham Watson, æt. 78. Gravel. He has left a widow and a son and daughter. A venerable old man.
112. July 17. Sarah Knight, æt. 32. Consumption. D. of Nath'l. A widow mother, two brothers and three sisters are survivors.
113. July 23. Lydia, d. of Thomas & Lydia Dean, æt. 2 years. Atrophia infantilis. Deformed. One son left.
114. August 4. Elizabeth, of Benjamin & Elizabeth Brown, æt. 4 months. Atrophia infantilis. No children left.
115. Aug. 6. Benj., s. of Benjamin & Susannah Dean, æt. 21 years. He was humpbacked and laboured under great infirmities.
116. Aug. 12. Margaret, of Joseph & Margaret Strout, æt. 15 months. Fever attending measles. They have one child, son, left and she one by former marriage.
117. Aug. 16. Mary Whittemore, æt. 19. Con-

sumption. She lived with her mother and the children. The father has absconded.

118. Aug. 17. Joseph Lambert; æt. 59, suddenly. He was a well known Master of a vessel. See Day Book.

119. Aug. 25. Peter, of Samuel & Elizabeth Murray, æt. 3, in the almshouse. Fever after measles. Six children left.

120. Aug. 26. Elisha, of John and Susannah Gunnison, æt. 16 months. After influenza and measles. Three children left.

121. Aug. 31. William, of John & Hannah Collins, æt. 17 months. Fever after measles. They have six children living, by the present wife.

122. Aug. 31. William, of William & Elizabeth Cotton, æt. 16 months. Dysentery. They have no other child. This child was for some time weak in the back, etc.

123. Sept. 3. Samuel Smith, æt. 77. Atroph. Senilis. A batchelor. He has left a maiden sister, who has lived 12 years with him in the Almshouse.

124. Sept. 7. Samuel, of Thomas & Elizabeth Chipman, æt. 14 months. Fever after measles. They have two sons left.

125. Sept. 26. Jonathan, of Henry & Sarah Prince, æt. 8 months. Fever after measles. They have a son and daughter left.

126. Sept. 28. Jonathan, of Samuel & Elizabeth Murray, æt. 6 months, of fever after measles. They have five children left. Almshouse.

127. Oct. 10. Rachel Odell, aged 84. A widow, she has left one son with 9 children. Almshouse.

128. Oct. 12. Ebenezer Burrill, æt. 7 years. A fever after measles. Son of Ebenezer & Mary, who live at Boston. The child died at its g. m. Wyatts.

129. Oct. 13. Jonathan Lander, Master of a vessel, æt. 44. He was seized with violent bleeding in the spring, and fell into a decay rapidly. A wife and one child. See Day Book.

130. Oct. 20. News of the death of Capt. Thomas Dean, jun'r, æt. 32. He died in Wilmington, No. Carolina, Oct. 3. Nervous fever. He has left a wife and two children, one male. See Day B.

131. Oct. 23. John Horton, æt. 34. Phthisick suddenly. He has left a wife, of the family of Grant, and two children, one male.

132. Nov. 2. Israel, s. of Joshua & Elizabeth Dodge, æt. 3 weeks. Suddenly, fever probably. They have four children left, one son.

133. Nov. 4. Samuel Odell, æt. 44. Consumption. He has left a wife and 9 children, 5 males. From the pest house on Neck.

134. Nov. 13. Male child of Samuel & Elizabeth Cashew, in a few hours after birth. The g. Father was a native Irishman.

135. Nov. 14. News of the death of John Nesboth, æt. 48. He died on board of Capt. Sam'l Derby in Port au Prince, West India Flux, Oct. 14th. He has left a wife dangerously sick. See D. B. 19.

136. Nov. 23. Elizabeth Cashew, alias Kehou, æt. 19, of puerperal fever. She has left an husband. She was a Browne.

137. Nov. 28. William, of James and Alice Cotton, æt. 2 years. Atrophia Infantilis. She has a child by a former husband.

138. Dec. 3. Female child of James & Judith Jeffry, within 3 hours of birth. They are lately married.

139. Dec. 17. Mary Whitefoot, aged 103. Atrop. Senilis. Known by the name of Granny W. She has left a daughter and g. children.

DEATHS FOR 1791.

140. Jan. 28. Daniel Shehane, æt. 46, of Ireland. He has left a wife and six male children. West India Flux, suddenly, in great pain.

141. Feb. 15. Cynthia, d. of Samuel & Lydia Woodkind, æt. 5 years, after lingering Phthisic in consumption. They have one daughter left.

142. Mar. 1. Lydia Smith, wife of Samuel Smith, æt. 67. She has had three husbands and has left three daughters. Atroph. Sen. See D. B.

143. Mar. 12. Abigail Nesboth, æt. 28. Consumption. She has left two sons, one by a former husband, and one at the breast.

144. Mar. 19. Sally, d. of William & Rebecca Fairfield, æt. 5 years, suddenly by an obstruction in the windpipe. Called widow, left with 6 children, 2 males.

145. Mar. 23. Son of Mercy Burke, æt. 7 days. Illegitimate. Atrophy. The g. Mother, mother and this daughter and 4 children together. She æt. 16.

146. Mar. 30. Violet Grant, æt. 37. Negro. See Day Book.

147. April 11. Elizabeth Jacobs, æt. 59. Bleeding from a cancer. Of the family of Hilliard. Married a Fry, then Jacobs, a daughter living by Fry.

148. April 16. George, s. of George & Lydia Hodges, æt. 4 years. Narrow chest. They have one child, a daughter.

149. April 16. Hannah Mansfield, suddenly, æt. 82. A widow and antient school dame. She has left an idiot daughter.

150. May 1. William, s. of Joshua & Esther French, æt. 3 months, of a fever attending chin cough. They have 3 children; 2 males.

151. May 3. Elizabeth, d. of Samuel & Susannah Ingersoll, æt. 4 years, of a fever attending chin cough. They have 3 children, 2 males.

152. May 10. Mercy White, widow. Consumption, æt. 41. She has left 5 children, one male.

153. May 14. John, s. of Francis & Mary Boardman, æt. 5 years. Consumption & grew deformed, was a fine child. They have 4 children, one son.

154. June 20. Sarah, d. of Richard & Sarah Hodges, æt. 5 years, mother a widow, only child. Fever with chin cough.

June 27. News by letter from the Captain.

155. William Dean, æt. 28, who perished off the Texall, mate on board of Capt. Henry Elkins, who alone survived of the crew on March 21.

156. Aaron Battern, æt. 26, in the same storm and vessel. He has left a wife and one child.

157. Samuel Bowditch, æt. 22, etc. He has left a wife and one child.

158. James Cotton, æt. 23. He has left a wife.

159. Samuel Shehane, æt. 17. His mother is a widow, and has five sons left.

160. Charles Williams, Swedish servant to Capt. Elkins, æt. 21.

This part of the crew of the Brig Harriette belonged to our Society.

161. June 29. Abigail, d. of Jonathan & Elizabeth Mason, æt. 2 months. Convulsions. They have three children, one son left.

162. June 30. News of the death of Capt. Nathaniel Silsbee, æt. 48. He died on ship board on the 25th, entering New York. A wife, four children, 3 sons.

163. July 7. News of the death of William Elkins,

æt. 19. He was knocked overboard in a high sea on 17 April in Capt. Loring.

164. July 9. News of the death of William Cotton, æt. 26. He died at Batavia in Java. He has left a widow. See Day Book.

165. July 2. News of the death of Capt. W. Carleton, æt. 46. He died at Barbadoes. He has left a second wife and a son. See Day Book. (Notes and usual ceremonies, but he was found to be alive.)

166. July 16. John, son of Benjamin & Margaret Nourse, æt. 3, of the cough with convulsions. They have 3 children, 2 boys.

167. } Aug. 15. Twin males of Thomas & Elizabeth
168. } Parsons, in 36 hours after birth. They have two children, one male.

169. Aug. 19. News of John Forbes, drowned in Virginia, æt. 28. He has left a wife and four children. Died in February. See Day Book.

170. Aug. 20. Henry, s. of John & Abigail Nesboth, 8 months. The father and mother both dead. Atrophy.

171. Sept. 17. Male child of William & Hannah Webb, soon after delivery. Their first child.

172. Sept. 26. Catherine Freeman, a Free Negro. Dropsy, &c., æt. 37. Husband Mingo and a son, formerly servant in Derby family.

173. Sept. 29. Abigail Archer, died after short illness, æt. 86. She lived with her son Jonathan. Left children.

174. Oct. 31. John Symonds, died of old age. See D. B. Æt. 100. A temperate, sober man. He has left a son and two daughters.

175. Nov. 28. Jonathan Ward, son of John, deceased. Fever, æt. 21. He died in the West Indies with Capt. Wellman, Oct. 20th.

176. Dec. 1. Mehitabel Archer, wife of Jonathan, jun'r, æt. 42. She has left 8 children, 3 males. Consumption.

177. Dec. 20. News of the death of Francis Grant, jun'r. Fever, æt. 25, on board Sinclair's Adeone, a Guinea vessel, in September. Mate. Left a wife and two children.

LIST OF DEATHS FOR 1792.

178. Jan. 21. John Ropes, old age, æt. 98. He lived with his g. son. Of an unquiet temper in his last years.

179. Jan. 24. Elizabeth Collins, widow. Delirious, æt. 63. She lived with her son, J. Fairfield. Was a Foot. One child, daughter, by James Murray living, and two daughters by Collins living.

180. Feb. 22. Michael, a freedman negro, worn out, æt. 55. Lived with F. Coombs and Jo. White, bred in Martinico. A good fellow. See D. B.

181. Mar. 16. News of the death of Capt. Francis Boardman. Fever, æt. 44. Left a wife and 4 children, one male. In Port au prince, Hispaniola, Feb. 10. See D. B.

182. Mar. 16. News of the death of George Dean. Fever, æt. 22. Left a wife and one child, male. In Port au Prince, Hispaniola, Feb. 14. See D. B.

183. Mar. 25. Susannah Saunders, wife of John. Consumption, æt. 31. Left five children, two males. She was a Mason. See D. B.

184. Mar. 27. Ebenezer Phippen. Bleeding and consumption, æt. 42. Left seven children and wife, 2 males. An example of extreme animal distress.

185. Apr. 30. Thomas Hunt, buried. Drowned, æt. 46. Left a wife and 5 children, one male. He was a Teacher of Navigation. See D. B.

186. June 7. Henry Parker buried. Drowned, æt. 34. Left a wife and 3 children, one male. Fisherman. See D. B.

187. June 8. Joseph Moses. Rheumatism, &c., æt. 23, at Mrs. Williams. Usher in the East Writing School.

188. June 8. Elizabeth Mason, wife of Jonathan. Mortification, æt. 35. Left three children, one male. Suddenly, tho' long complaining.

189. June 12. Hannah Burns, widow. Consumption, æt. 34. Left four children, two males. After an unhappy life. See D. B.

190. June 25. News of the death of John Dean, Apr. 30. Drowned at sea, æt. 20. Son of Benjn. They have four left, one male. He was with his father. See D. B.

191. June 27. News of the death of Neal Antony Wiederberg. Drowned at sea, æt. 17. A Swede. Apprentice of Capt. Clifford Byrne.

192. July 20. Sarah Hodges, widow of Richard. Consumption, æt. 30. She was a Chever. No child left. At her sister Boardman's.

193. July 27. Nathaniel, of William and R. King. Convulsions, æt. 2 mos. Mother a Phippen. After a long time.

194. July 27. William, of Johnson & Ruth Briggs, News of. Fever, æt. 20. Eldest son, died July 12. At Guadeloupe Point Pierre.

195. Aug. 11. James Jeffry, s. of Arthur. W. India Flux, æt. 26. Left a wife. Returned sick from W. Indies with S. Ingersoll.

196. Aug. 21. Mary Berry, wife of John. Consumption, æt. 56. Left two children, one male. She was a Putnam. See D. B.

197. Sept. 29. Margaret, of Thomas & Hannah Keen.

Vomiting and P., æt. 11 months. No child living by first wife. She married a Cox, a former husband.

198. Oct. 6. News of the death of Joseph English. Fever, æt. 22. Son of Philip. He died in Maryland.

199. Oct. 9. Hannah, of Benjamin & Hannah Hodges. Consumption, æt. 13. They have two sons and two d's left. Father in the East Indies.

200. Oct. 9. Male child of Matthew & Sarah Vincent at delivery. Their first child. A forced delivery in a critical case.

201. Oct. 11. Richard Deighton. W. India Flux, æt. 47. He married a Whittemore. Has left neither wife nor child.

202. Oct. 15. Lydia Beadle. Consumption, æt. 47. She has left 4 sons and a daughter. Lived long a widow with reputation.

203. Oct. 20. Peggy, d. of M. General Fiske. Consumption, æt. 17. Three sisters and a bro. left. The second daughter lost by the same disorder.

204. Oct. 22. Mary Knight, d. of Sarah. Consumption, æt. 24. Two brothers and two sisters. Mother long a widow.

205. Oct. 26. John White, Captain. Complication of disorders, æt. 70. Left five daughters. Long confined and debilitated.

206. Oct. 28. Samuel, s. of Richard Valpy, jun'r. Small pox, æt. 10. In the natural way, full.

207. Nov. 1. James Beverley, s. in law of Frank Telbert. Small pox, æt. 22. African race. In the natural way, full.

208. Nov. 4. Male child of Oliver Webb. Convulsions, æt. 48 hours. Three children, 2 males. *She* was an Elkins. A fine child.

209. Nov. 6. News of the death of Captain Christo-

pher Babbidge. W. India Flux, æt. 51. A wife and four children, 2 males. Died Aug. 26, at St. Sebastian's, Spain.

210. Nov. 6. Richard Collins, of Kingston, N. Hampshire. Fever, æt. 27. An only child, with C. Patterson, died in the offing on return-from W. Indies.

211. Nov. 24. Judith, wife of Timothy Wellman. Small pox, æt. 22. She was a Bowditch, husband at sea, in the natural way.

212. Nov. 13. Ruth, d. of Benjamin Chever. Small pox, æt. 20. Oldest child by former wife. By inoculation.

213. Dec. 7. Mary, d. of Ebenezer & Elizabeth Phippen. Atrophy, æt. 11 months. Widow. With 6 children, 2 males, unprovided for.

214. Dec. 11. Male child of Thomas & Hannah Vincent. Convulsions, æt. 12 days. Their first and only child. Living with her mother Cloutman.

DEATHS IN 1793.

215. Jan. 8. Elizabeth, widow of John McGrew. Palsy, æt. 63. She was a Cloutman. Six weeks after the first shock.

216. Feb. 15. News of the d. of Edward Crowninshield. Fever, æt. 17. Son of George Crowninshield. At Guataloupe, W. Indies.

217. Mar. 26. Male child of Samuel & Lydia Leach, still born. He was their first child. They had funeral ceremonies.

218. Apr. 14. Sarah Diman, wife of Thomas, m. 30 yrs. Dropsy, æt. 67.

219. Apr. 16. Joanna Silsbee, widow of William.

Age, æt. 80. She was of the fam. Fowle. She had been a widow 14 years. 3 daughters.

220. May 3. Mary Lander, widow of ———. Age, æt. 88. She was a Bason of Boston. She had been a widow above 30 years. 2 daughters.

221. May 16. Betsey, of Jonathan & Mehitable Archer. Atrophy, æt. 2. Their youngest child. Sick mother, who died in the year of its birth.

222. June 29. Elizabeth, wife of Thomas Williams. King's Evil, 35. Left two children, one by Mr. Symmes. Long sickness. She was a Swasey.

223. July 16. George Logan, M.D. Edinb. Decay, æt. 45. Left a wife and four children in Charleston, S.C. At Capt. Allen's for his health. See

224. July 16. Hannah MacGregory. Consumption, æt. 32. No children, but a husband at sea. She was a Silsbee. He Scotchman.

225. July 25. Roger, Negroman in the service of Capt. Allen. Drowned, æt. 27. From the family estate of Mrs. Allen. Bringing up a boat for a party next day.

226. Aug. 4. Mercy, daughter of Benjn. Marston. Consumption, æt. 22. Lingering since small pox, natural way.

227. Aug. 12. William Lord, Berwick mariner. Fever, æt. 25. He has a mother, died at Silsbee's. Came sick into port from W. Ind., with Millet.

228. Sept. 6. William Patterson, Capt., mariner. W. Ind. flux, æt. 47. Left a wife and four children, one daughter. Came sick from W. Ind. *A worthy man.*

229. Sept. 13. Female child of Eleanora Odell. Atrophy, æt. 19 mos.

230. Oct. 8. Sarah Gibaut, w. of Edward. Disentery, æt. 63. They have one son abroad. She was a Crowninshield.

231. Oct. 11. Walter Palfrey. Age, æt. 73. He has one surviving daughter. He was bedridden many months.
232. Oct. 20. Elizabeth, widow of Thomas Welcome. Fever, æt. 28. She was a Lambert. Has left two, her own children, son and daughter.
233. Nov. 1. News of death of Robert Phippen. Fever, æt. 29. He was from Waterford, Ireland; left a wife and three children; married eleven years. Died in West Indies.
234. Nov. 6. News of death of William Peele. Fever, æt. 21. Second son of William Peele. Died in West Indies, first voyage.

DEATHS IN 1794.

235. Feb. 3. Elizabeth Murray, widow of Samuel. Bleeding, 70. Has left children, died in a few minutes. Gyllingham.
236. Feb. 8. Female child of Samuel & Sally Waters. Delivery, few hours. They have one living daughter. Young family.
237. Feb. 16. Mary Burroughs. Consumption, æt. 43. Has left children by different [husbands]. Stileman.
238. Feb. 20. Mary, wife of Capt. Thomas Dean. Rheumatism, æt. 67. Has left two daughters, one single. Long confinement. She a Cash.
239. Feb. 22. News of the death of Capt. Johnson Briggs. Fever, æt. 45. A wife and nine children, three daughters. He was from Taunton.
240. Mar. 10. News of death of Edward Shehane. Died Jan. 16. Fever, æt. 19. A widow mother, etc. At Aux Cayes, Hisp. Go. Hodges, Capt.
241. Mar. 15. News of death of Andrew Preston.

Died Dec. 6 (?). Fever, æt. 22. Parents living, etc. On voyage to Cape de Verd Islands. Capt. Holt.

242. Apr. 11. Mary, widow of William Browne. Aged, æt. 80. Living with her son William, only surviving child. Sick about a week. A Frost.

243. Apr. 14. Abigail Masury, widow. Complication, æt. 65. Left a daughter. Lame and infirm a long time. A Webb.

244. Apr. 18. News of William, son of William Thomas. Fever, æt. 15. Father long absent. Died abroad in West Indies with Capt. J. Briggs.

245. May 3. Sarah, wife of James Collins. Fever, æt. 64. Left four children, two sons married. A Thomas.

246. ———. Rebeccah, daughter of B. Gale. Epilepsy, æt. 22. Two sisters living, parents dead. Deformed, etc., through life.

247. June 5. Mary Crowninshield, widow. Consumption, æt. 67. She was an Ives. Left a son and five daughters. Long sickness and infirmity.

248. June 6. James Collins. Fever, æt. 61. Left four children, two sons married. Buried his wife last month.

249. June 25. Mary, of Samuel & Rebecca Silsbee. Fever, æt. 5. Their second child, three living. After a few days' illness.

250. ———. Elizabeth, of Thomas & Elizabeth Chipman. Fever, æt. 4. Their third child, three living. Mortification in the bowels.

251. July 9. Mary, of William & Lydia Peele. Atrophy, æt. 4 months. Mother dying in consumption. Father dead before its birth.

252. July 18. Elizabeth, wife of William Foye. Consumption, æt. 39. Has left nine children, four males. Ulcers in the lungs, as her sister. A Masury.

253. Aug. 4. Lydia Peele. Consumption, æt. 25. Intended husband and child dead. Daughter of Nurse Peele so called.

254. Aug. 12. Female child of George & Hannah Taylor. Still born. Daughter of Nurse Peele, and 4th death this year. Their first child.

255. Aug. 26. Joseph Crookshanks. Consumption, æt. 47. Married Widow Newhall. 1786. Native of London, England.

256. Oct. 1. Anna, daughter of Penn & Anna Townsend. Consumption, æt. 22. Mother died same day, eight years before. Last child of the family.

257. Oct. 9. Ruth Squires, daughter of Ruth Newton. Vomiting and purging, æt. 43. A husband and one daughter.

258. Oct. 25. Phippen, of Stephen & Sarah Hill. Quincy, æt. 13 months. Their only child. She was a Crane.

259. Nov. 3. Priscilla, of Samuel & Elizabeth Masury. Quincy, æt. 4 years. Four children, one daughter. She was d. of St. Webb.

260. Nov. 3. Benjamin Henderson, a batchelor. Fever sore, æt. 59. He has been bedridden four years.

261. Nov. 6. Thomas Lazell Whitehead. Rheumatism, æt. 17. G. son of Lazell's wife, and adopted by him. Four years afflicted by rheumatism.

262. Nov. 14. Eliza, of George & Lydia Hodges. Quincy. 6 years. They have two children, one male. After long complaints.

263. Nov. 18. John MacGregory, Capt., Mariner. Consumption, æt. 34. Native of Edinburg. No child. Wife died July, 1793. He died at York.

264. Nov. 23. Rebecca, of William & Rebecca Che-

ver. Quincy, æt. 2 years, 7 months. They have no child left. She was a Whitford.

265. Nov. 30. News of the death of Benjamin Knights, at sea. Fever, æt. 18. Son of widow Sarah, of Nathaniel. From West Indies, Nov. 4, voyage home.

266. Dec. 6. News of the death of Benjamin Bowditch, at sea. Fever, æt. 22. Only son of widow Mary. Died 2 Dec., from West Indies. Shillaber, buried in M. Vineyard.

267. Dec. 11. Sarah Martin. Consumption, æt. 55. Daughter of Mayberry. Husband a Portuguese, where unknown.

268. Dec. 12. News of the death of William Wyatt. Fever, æt. 34. Left a wife and three children. Died at New Orleans.

269. Dec. 13. News of the death of Stephen, son of David Smith. Fever, æt. 16. His mother married Sage. Died in the West Indies.

DEATHS IN 1795.

270. Jan. 15. News of the d. of Capt. Benj. Orne. Fever, æt. 28. He has a mother, &c., at York. Abroad in W. Indies.

271. ———. James, of John & Ruth Collins. Quincy, æt. 3 years. They have four children, two sons. This death within 24 hours of complaint.

272. Jan. 20. John Smith, native of Ipswich. Fever, æt. 28. Left a wife and two children. Died at Boston, on his return from W. Indies. Buried at Salem. See Day Book.

273. ———. Caroline, of Joseph and Mary Waters. Fever, æt. 13 months. They have five daughters left. No apprehensions of imm. danger.

274. Jan. 23. Elizabeth, of William & Jane Wyatt. Quincy, æt. 27 months. Two children left, one son. The widow is not a native.

275. Feb. 6. News of the death of Jonathan Elkins. Fever, æt. 17. Son of John & Sarah. Mother Taylor on board Capt. Josiah Orne, W. Indies.

276. Feb. 24. Daniel Staniford, of Nathaniel & Abigail Rogers. Fever, æt. 4 months. They have 4 boys left. Long sickness.

277. April 19. Samuel Dodd, born in Marblehead. Palsy, æt. 30. Wife and two children. Distressing sickness. See Day Book, XXIII.

278. May 9. News of the d. of Capt. Henry Phillips. Fever, Apr. 15, æt. 24. A mother and one sister. In Cape Francois Domingo detained.

279. May 4. Of Jonathan Perkins, Br. of Tarrant Perkins. Fever, æt. 19. Born in Middleton. On a West India Voyage.

280. May 2. Of William Becket, son of Mary. Fever, March 15, æt. 18. A mother with two children, one son. First voyage with C. Lee in Grenada.

281. May 13. Of Samuel Byrne, on board Capt. R. Crowninshield. Drowned, æt. 13. Two sisters and a brother at home, was with his G. G. mother Archer.

282. May 24. William, of Ebenezer & Sally Sloacum. Fever, æt. 10 months. She a Becket. He not of Salem. They have one child, a son, left.

283. ———. Rebecca Smith, widow of Samuel. Fever, æt. 63. She was a Lovett of Beverly. She has left two daughters married.

284. June 4. Jonathan Millet, Sen. Fever, æt. 60. Left a widow and seven children, three daughters. Four of his children married.

285. June 9. Eliza, d. of Robert & Anstis Stone. Debility, æt. 9 years. Three daughters and two sons left. She grew exceedingly deformed.

286. July 4. Samuel, of Cornelius & Grace Bartlett. Vomiting and purging, æt. 12 months. Only child, young family. They have been three years from Marblehead.

287. July 19. Margaret Murray, wife of Peter. Consumption, æt. 44. She was a d. of Stephen Webb. She has left only one child, a daughter.

288. ———. News of d. of Samuel Rhue, s. of Thomas. Fever, æt. 14. They have seven children, four males. At Port au Prince, with Capt. B. Dean.

289. ———. News of d. of Samuel Waters. Fever, æt. 31. Left a wife and two daughters. On his return homeward from W. Indies.

290. Aug. 16. Mary Newhall. Fever, æt. 14. A mother and three brothers. After a few days illness.

291. Aug. 27. Sarah, of John & Ruth Collins. Fever, æt. 12 months. They have three children, two males. After a few days illness.

292. Aug. 31. John Stephens. Bleeding with fever, æt. 15 years. An apprentice to Joseph Vincent. Belonging to Kittery, Me.

293. Sept. 14. Hannah, of James & Hannah Collins. Fever, æt. 3 years. Three children, two males left. Short sickness. Scarlet fever, etc.

294. Sept. 23. Ruth, of Oliver & Sarah Webb. Fever, 8 months. They have three children left, one daughter. Short sickness, all children been sick.

295. ———. Joseph Prince, of Daniel & Deborah Sage. Fever, 18 months. They have three children, one daughter. All the children sick.

296. ———. Elizabeth, wife of Joseph Vincent.

Fever, etc., æt. 64. There are three sons and four daughters. Fever, with dropsy and palsy and long lameness.

297. Sept. 24. Margaret, wife of Tarrant Perkins. Fever, æt. 18. Married five months since. A tender frame, after short illness. A Chever.
These fevers with inflamed throat.

298. Sept. 26. Daniel, of Daniel & Deborah Sage. Fever, æt. 4 years. One son and one daughter left. Second child lost in one week.

299. ———. News of the death of William Dunlap. Fever, æt. 20. From Ireland, one year in America, with Capt. Berry at Hispaniola.

300. ———. News of the death of John Dale. Fever, æt. 32. A wife and two children, one son. Mariner, with Capt. Berry, on his passage homeward.

301. Oct. 1. William, of Samuel & Susannah Archer. Fever, æt. 2 years, 3 months. Two children left, one son. The fever was attended with mortification.

302. Oct. 4. Hannah, of Daniel & Deborah Sage. Fever, æt. 6 years. Only one son left. Three have died in eleven days.

303. Oct. 13. Gamaliel, of Gamaliel & Sarah Hodges. Fever, æt. 3 years, 8 months. Two sons left. Hard struggle, short illness.

304. Oct. 15. Hannah, wife of William Becket. Fever, æt. 22. No child, married one year. She was a Butler. Sick five days.

305. Oct. 16. Mary, of James & Sarah Richardson. Fever, æt. 7 years. Two sons left; she a widow. Sick three days, attended with mortification.

306. Oct. 20. Maria, of Walter & Susannah Jeffrey. Vomiting and purging, æt. 14 months. She was a Smith, Two daughters left. Sick a month, died at last in fits.

307. Oct. 21. Nathaniel, of Jonathan & Mary Andrew. Fever, æt. 18. Mother widow, three sisters, two brothers. Confined a fortnight, complaining thirty days.

308. Nov. 1. John, of Andrew & Martha Ward. Fever, æt. 9 months. One male child left. Sick a fortnight.

309. Nov. 5. Martha, of William & Eunice Burrill. Fever, æt. 6 years. Two children left, one male. Sick three weeks. Mother a Coffin.

310. Nov. 8. Samuel, of Thomas & Lydia Masury. Convulsions, æt. 2 years. Two children left, males. Sick and apparently upon recovery before death.

311. Nov. 11. Mary, of David & Mary Martin. Worms, æt. 18 months. One child left, a female. He from Ipswich. She a Bowditch. Sick a week.

312. Nov. 12. News of the death of Pearce Evoy. Drowned, æt. 35. A wife and three children, one male. He from Ireland. She a Richardson. Married nine years.

313. Nov. 26. Hannah, of Joseph & Hannah Hosmer. Fever and throat, æt. 2 years and 10 months. Two children left, one male. He from Norwich, Conn. Sick a fortnight.

314. Nov. 28. News of the death of Thomas Keen. Fever, æt. 45. He has left a wife and one child by himself. He was from Halifax, Nova Scotia, and died (last time married nine years) at Dunkirk, 28 Dec., 1794.

315. Dec. 1. Mary, of Joseph and Hannah Hosmer. Fever and throat, æt. 1 year and 4 months. Only one son left; the other daughter died Nov. 26.

316. Dec. 7. Patty, of Samuel & Lydia[1] Odell. Fever and throat, æt. 10. Nine children upon death of the

---

[1]Lois written over Lydia by Dr. Bentley as though not quite certain which was right.

father, but now much scattered and life uncertain. This child grew deformed from an accident.

317. Dec. 10. News of the death of Jonathan Webb. Fever, æt. 27. A mother, brother, and two sisters. He was carried into Hisp. A mate of Capt. Martin.

318. Dec. 14. Female. child of John & Hannah Mac. Contusion in the head, æt. 3 weeks. Lately married. She a Beadle. Child feeble from birth, etc.

319. Dec. 17. Mary Wardilloe; family name Thomas. Old age, æt. 77. Her first husband a Nourse. Twice married. She has been midwife at above 1200 births; died in the Charity House.

320. Dec. 19. Lydia Newhall, wife of David. Fever, æt. 25. She was a Clary, married nineteen months. Left a child, female. Husband at sea.

321. Dec. 21. Thomas Diman. Old age, æt. 74. He has left a daughter and grand children. He fell into the fire not long before death.

322. Dec. 24. Mercy, of William & Mary Ropes. Fever, nerv. and putr., æt. 8 years and 6 months. They have left six children, two males. This 2nd daughter. Father at sea.

323. Dec. 26. Mary, of Benjamin & Hannah Gardner. Fever, æt. 10 months. They have five children, two males.

324. Dec. 30. Mary Lambert. Old age, æt. 90. Been a widow years. Left five children and twenty-six grand-children and sixty great-grand-children.

325. Dec. 31. Hannah Ward, d. of John. Fever and consumption, æt. 18. Parents dead. Has four brothers and one sister.

326. ———. News of the death of David Martin. Fever, æt. 29. Died at Hispaniola; left a wife and one child, female. Belonged to Ipswich.

327. ———. News of the death of David Newhall. Fever, æt. 27. Wife lately deceased. Left one child, female. Died at Hispaniola.

DEATHS IN 1796.

328. Jan. 2. Mary Thompson, widow-in-law. Dysentery mt., æt. 36. She was a Smith; no children.

329. Jan. 15. Mary, of William & Mary Ropes. Dropsy in the head, æt. 11. Five left, two sons. The physicians agreed upon this case.

330. Jan. 15. Susannah Masury, maiden, æt. 65. She has sisters living. In the Charity House. A Pilgrim.

331. Jan. 24. Elizabeth, wife of George Perkins. Cancer, æt. 40. Ten years married. She has left three children, two males, in great poverty. Neglect of husband. Born in Marblehead.

332. Jan. 25. Nathaniel Richardson. Killed by a moving house, æt. 54. Twenty-four years married. He has left six children, one daughter. He was assisting to remove a building. Born at Woburn.

333. Feb. 2. John Symonds, a batchelor. Age, æt. 74. He has left a sister with whom he lived. His father died at 100, in Oct., 1791.

334. Feb. 3. Mercy Smith, a maiden. Age, æt. 85. She had a brother Benjamin, with whom she lived twelve years in the Charity House, who died in 1790.

335. Feb. 3. Male child of Thomas & Rebecca Alexander. 6 months. Both parents in the Charity House, not of our Society. Strangers. He from Ireland.

The last two buried together.

336. Feb. 4. News of the death of Joshua Foster. Fever, æt. 29. One and a half years married. He was

a native of Ipswich, married a Holt. Died 6 of Dec., in West Indies; mate of a Capt. Patten's vessel.

337. Feb. 8. Priscilla, daughter of Thomas & Priscilla Welcome. Consumption, æt. 19. Her parents died young in consumption. Two own sisters and one sister and brother-in-law. Her mother a Webb. She died at her grandfather's, Step. Webb.

338. Feb. 20. Mary Walker, wife of John. He absent. Dropsy, æt. 42. 1st marriage, five years; 2nd marriage, eleven years. She was a Whitefoot. Two sisters, no children. Her first husband MacDonald. She died at Capt. Clifford Byrnes.

339. Feb. 26. News of the death of Laura, youngest daughter of Samuel & Priscilla Lambert. Quincy, upon measles, 12 months. One child, female, left. She was upon a visit to Scarborough, Dunstan.

340. March 10. News of the death of George Syms, died Feb. 17. Fever, æt. 12. He was at Aux Cayes with his father-in-law Williams. Both his own parents dead.

341. March 12. News of the death of Samuel Swasey. Fever, æt. 30. Three years married. He has left a wife and one child, male. In the East Indies, Calcutta, with G. G. Smith.

342. March 24. Stephen Webb, of an antient family. Gravel and rupture and asthma, æt. 74. 1st marriage, one year; 2nd marriage, twenty-five years; 3d marriage, 4 years. He has left two sons and five daughters, children by second wife. 1st marriage, Best; 2nd marriage, Tyler, widow Manning; 3d marriage, Beans, widow Masury.

343. Mar. 28. William, of Joseph & Mary Brown. Sudden, æt. 6 months. They have four children, three sons, left. She was a Becket; has four sisters and two brothers married, one brother unmarried.

344. Mar. 31. Rebecca, wife of Thomas Williams. After delivery, æt. 25. 1st marriage, five years, He; 2nd marriage, one and a half years, She. She was a Smith and her first child. W's second wife; first wife married five years, a Swasey.

345. Apr. 21. Male child of Benjamin & Hannah Webb. Still-born. She was a Bray. Five children, four males. There were funeral solemnities.

346. May 18. Josiah Gaines, a truly worthy man. Gout in stomach, æt. 76. Fifty years married. He was born in Ipswich; lived in Boston, a rope maker, till 1775. He was afflicted with the gout forty years. His wife of Boston, infirm.

347. May 19. News of Jonathan Archer, son of John. Fever, æt. 23. His parents, five brothers, and three sisters, survive. Died in April in Hispaniola.

348. June 4. Mary, widow of Capt. Benj. Bates. Dropsy, æt. 71. Thirty-six years married. Left one surviving daughter; lived a widow twelve years; great poverty relieved by friends. A Dolbeare.

349. June 18. News of the death of Nathaniel Phippen. Drowned, æt. 17. Son of Nathaniel & Abigail Phippen. Drowned off Cape of Good Hope, 4 Jan., from on board Capt. Chipman.

350. July 4. Samuel, of Samuel & Sarah Kehou. Dysentery, v. and p., 6 months. Their only child. She a Ruee. Father at sea.

351. July 13. Lydia, wife of George Hodges. Childbed, æt. 32. Ten years married. She was a Gale. Left son and daughter and one sister. She was very infirm. See xxxi.

352. Aug. 23. John, of William & Jane Wyatt. Worm fever, æt. 8. She is not a native of these states.

One son left. She lost her husband in 1794 and her only daughter in Jan., 1795.

353. Aug. 28. Benjamin Marston. Mortification in the bowels, etc., æt. 62. 35 years married. His wife is living in the Charity House, delirious. He has two daughters left. He was not of our Society. Died in the Charity House.

354. Aug. 29. James Leslie. Dysentery, etc., æt. 22. He was born in New York and has there a stepmother and sisters. He was very irregular and never lived in the town. Died in the Charity House.

355. Sept. 5. News of the death of Stephen, of John Webb. Fever, abroad, æt. 23. His father, mother, four brothers and sister living. He died 6 Aug., upon his homeward passage from Batavia with his brother Benj.

356. Oct. 2. Mary, of John & Mary Berry. Worms, 15 months. They have three male children. She was a Ward.

357. Oct. 4. Abigail Laskin, a maiden. Dysentery, æt. 73. Of small capacity, but inoffensive. She died in the Charity House.

358. Oct. 16. Penn Townsend, Captain. Drowned, æt. 63. 1st marriage, 30 years; 2nd marriage, 10 years. He has left a second wife; children dead; one grandchild living. He was drowned from a coasting vessel (Jno. Archer, Capt.) off Nahant, upon his return from Boston.

359. Nov. 10. News of the death of Joseph, of Joseph Lambert. Fever, abroad, æt. 14. One son and three daughters left. Died from the vessel of his father, who was with him at Aux Cayes.

360. Nov. 18. Sarah, wife of William Wyatt. Age, etc., æt. 70. Forty years married. Husband and three

daughters left. She was a Chever. For many years separated from her husband.

361. Dec. 10. William Wyatt. Age, etc., æt. 67. Forty years married. Husband of the above Sarah, born in Newbury.

362. Dec. 11. News of the death of Benjamin Sullivan. Fever, abroad, æt. 16. His father was from Ireland, named Timothy. Died on his voyage in W. Indies in Capt. Willis. Only child; mother a Swasey; long a widow.

363. Dec. 11. Henry, of James & Sarah Browne. Vomiting, 5 months. They have four children left, two males. Child infirm, but not long in danger.

364. Dec. 20. Male child of Samuel & Lydia Leach, soon after birth. 4 weeks. One child, a daughter, left. She was a Becket.

365. Dec. 28. Hannah, widow of Peter Murray. Palsy, æt. 72. Six years married. One son left by Murray. A female by Wormstead living. She was a Slate. Her mother a Becket. Lived a widow forty-five years. Sister living.

366. Dec. 31. Joseph Reinar, a Spaniard. Consumption, æt. 40. Had a wife and children. Came with Capt. Welsh; had been here a few weeks at S. Silsbee's.

DEATHS IN 1797.

367. Jan. 24. Robert Bartlet. Mariner, æt. 57. Thirty-six years married. He has left five children, one male and four females. A man of very disorderly mind. His wife was a Searle. He born in Marblehead.

368. Feb. 16. News of the death of Reuben Shad. Drowned, æt. 27. Five years married. He has left a wife, Catherine Coffin, and two male children, and she

with child. He was washed overboard from Capt. B. Dean on his outward bound voyage. The mate. Came from Billerica.

369. ———. And of David Malcom. Drowned, æt. 42. Fifteen years married. He has left a wife, an Ulmer, and four children, females. Mr. D. Malcolm suffered with Mr. Shad. Came from Warren, Maine. His wife a widow Becket, descended from so many, see. She has five living children by Becket, one daughter.

370. Mar. 2. Female child of Jona. and Elizabeth Millet, at birth. She was a Masury, three male children. Died soon after safe delivery.

371. Mar. 4. Mary, of Samuel & Rebecca Silsbee. Dropsy in the head, 10 months. She was a Reed, of Danvers. Three children, one male. These cases are doubtful.

372. Apr. 2. John, of James & Elizabeth Archer. Worms, æt. 2 and 8 months. They have four children, males. The child had recovered of the measles.

373. Apr. 4. Eunice Flint, maiden, of Danvers. Consumption, æt. 65. She lived with her niece, wife of S. Silsbee, jun., who was a Reed. She has lived in Salem two years only.

374. Mar. 20. News of the death of Capt. John Carnes, at Cape of Good Hope. Variorum, æt. 41. Fifteen years married. He married Lydia Derby, much against the will of Capt. R. Derby. His conduct proved unfavorable to his hopes. He left no children behind him. Died 12 December last.

375. Apr. 14. Robert, of Robert & Hannah Peele. Measles, æt. 3 years, 4 months. They have two children left, one male. The first of the measles this year. Measles about.

376. May 3. Male child of James & Mary Very, at

birth. They have two children, one son. She was a Palfrey by Warwick Palfrey's second wife.

377. June 3. Elizabeth, widow of Benja. Stone. Palsy, æt. 74. Eighteen years married. A son and daughter survive, R. Stone and E. White. She was a Berry, been a widow thirty-six years; married 1743. Husband lost at sea.

378. June 7. Benjamin Gardiner. Dropsy, æt. 77. 1st marriage, forty years; 2nd marriage, five years; a son and daughter Hitchins survive by first wife. He was of Boston, married 1751. Lived and married in Marblehead 2nd time; there two years. Thence to Salem, lived here twenty years. See Day Book.

379. June 9. Henry Hiller, of Philadelphia. Dysentery, æt. 22. Has a mother living; came sick from West Indies. Brought into this port by Capt. Joshua Richardson in May last and died in the Charity House.

380. July 4. Benjamin Cloutman, suddenly, in bed, æt. 48. Eighteen years married; has left a wife and eight children, four males. His wife was a Frye, granddaughter of Frye at Fort Anne. His mother was a Webb, daughter of Deacon Webb. Went to bed well, died in bed before his wife could see him.

381. July 6. Female child of Retire & Rebecca Becket. Fever, æt. 16 months. One child, male, left. She was a Swasey.

382. July 21. Samuel Ingersoll, jun., Capt. Consumption, æt. 22. Of Samuel & Susannah, parents living, a brother and sister left. He has been several voyages and had been confined seven months.

383. July 27. Eliza, of Edward & Elizabeth Archer. Convulsions, 12 months. Married a short time; only child. She a Phippen. Child taken in fits and died in a few hours.

384. Aug. 28. Jonathan Archer, senior. Consumption, æt. 65. 1st marriage, eighteen years; 2nd marriage, twenty-four years. Has left his second wife, two males and three females, the first, and one male and one female, the second. He was our Barber, and has been complaining for many years. He had a long and distressing sickness. First wife a Very; second a Silsbee.

385. Sept. 7. News of the death of Capt. John Waters. Fever, abroad, æt. 42. Six years married. Has left a wife and three children, one male and two females. She an English, one child by a former marriage. He sailed from Baltimore and died five days after his return, 13 Aug., from Hispaniola, at Baltimore.

386. Sept. 11. George Lassell, a mariner. Palsy, æt. 62. 1st marriage, — years; 2nd marriage, eighteen years. He was from Rhode Island state. He left America last war, '59; was married in England; had two children; wife deceased before his return. Has left a widow and no children in America. She was a widow Crispin, family Swasey.

387. Sept. 14. Hannah, wife of James Collins. Consumption, æt. 39. Eighteen years married. She was a Masury, mother survives. Has left three children, one daughter. She was sick and complaining about two years; a very worthy woman.

388. Sept. 26. A male child of Nell Odell. Canker, æt. 11 months.

389. Sept. 28. Major General John Fisk. Apoplexy, æt. 53. 1st marriage, sixteen years; 2nd marriage, two years; 3d marriage, ten years. Children only by first wife. Wife, a son and two daughters survived him. 1st wife a Phippen, 2nd a Lee, 3rd a Wendell, Widow Servy. A most noble man, son of Rev. S. Fisk of this town. A few years before his death he was deranged. The public experience a loss in his death.

390. Sept. 30. John Masury, blind with age, æt. 82. 1st marriage, thirty-five years; 2nd marriage, twenty-one years. Has left a wife and three children, one son. Both wives only children of brothers Bush; 2nd wife married Phippen, Bagnall, then Masury. He has been blind seven years. Followed the seas and bedridden from a fall.

391. Sept. 29. Hannah, wife of Joshua Pitman, mort. in bowels, æt. 40. Eighteen years married. She was a Sloaly of this town. Left three children, one female.

392. Oct. 11. Elizabeth, relict of Abraham Watson. Old age; suddenly, æt. 86. Fifty-four years married. She was a Pickering. Left a son and daughter. She lived with her son, John Watson, and in company with her sister, Mary Gardiner, æt. 82.

393. Oct. 13. News of the death of George Churd. Dysentery, W. Indies, æt. 39. Six years married. He married the widow Hodgden, who was a Masury; had no children. He was from Bristol, England. Died on his passage from the W. Indies, three days out of Port, with Capt. Moulton, of Beverly.

394. Oct. 17. Elizabeth, wife of Capt. Benjamin Ward. Complication, etc., æt. 60. Twenty-seven years married. She was a Babbidge, of John. Left no children. Long sick and complaining. Great fondness for Natural History; ever in her garden; of strong passions. Inclined to dropsy; died in a decay.

395. Oct. 22. Benjamin Waters. Fever, complication, æt. 47. Twenty years married; left six children, three sons. Married a Dane, who was delirious and died before him. Fever sore which never healed, etc., not of our Society. Lived several years in Beverly. Died at his mother's at the bridge.

396. Oct. 23. Mary Valpy, widow of John. Dysentery, æt. 62. Twenty-two years married. Left three

daughters; widow Stephens and Mrs. Crelly and one unmarried. She was a Masury, of Samuel. Had a paralytic shock, but finally much emaciated.

397. Nov. 30. John, of Benjamin & Hannah Hodges. Consumption, æt. 10. They have one son and four daughters left. Apparently rugged, but always feeble lungs; began to fail after the measles in the spring.

398. Dec. 1. News of Samuel Murray. Drowned, æt. 22. His mother Eliza is yet living and has four sons and a daughter left. Second son of Samuel. Fell overboard the first day after leaving this port on board of Capt. Daniel Ropes.

399. Dec. 5. Mary Renough, widow of Michael. Aged, æt. 92. Twenty-two years married. She has left one grandson. She was an Abbot; from her ancestors the Cove on the Neck so named. She lived with her daughter-in-law, the widow of Penn Townsend in Turner's street. Mortification. Her husband, from Isle of Jersey, killed by Indians, fishing, Oct., 1754.

400. Dec. 5. Thomas Vaicou of Guernsey. Suddenly, æt. 54. He lived with J. Phippen, then with Heald; buried from the Charity House; complained of a cold. He belonged to Marblehead and came young from Guernsey, went on crutches, suffered from a fever sore, died suddenly.

401. Dec. 6. Jacob Norman, a Swede. Drowned, æt. 42. Three years married. He married the widow Gunnison, who was an Archer, and had one child by her, a daughter. He was owner in part of a sloop coasting between Boston and Salem, and fell over coming down below the Castle.

402. Dec. 23. Lydia, widow of Robert Phippen. Consumption, æt. 32. Nine years married. She was a Valpy and grand-daughter of our former sexton Clough;

left three children, two sons. Her husband died in the Southern states four years ago, æt. 31. He was a foreigner, English, and died a mate on board of R. Derby's ship. Both not of our Society.

DEATHS IN 1798.

403. Jan. 4. Lydia, widow of Joseph King. Atroph. sen., æt. 66. Thirty-three years married. Left four sons and a daughter; one son in Nova Scotia at Cape Negro; one daughter in Eastham, Cape Cod; three sons in Salem. She was a Sparrow, born at Eastham, Barnstable Co., Mass. Removed to Barrington, Nova Scotia, and thence to Salem, twenty-three years since. Husband dead fifteen years.

404. Jan. 8. Hannah, of Richard & Susannah Valpy. Nervous fever, aged 10. They have four children, one daughter. The mother from Marblehead. His family has been some branches of it the most eccentric. This child had not seasonable aid.

405. Jan. 22. Mercy, widow of Thomas Masury. Fever, æt. 79. 1st marriage, two years; 2nd marriage, forty-seven years. She was a Legro; married at first William Matthews, and then Masury. She has left one son and one daughter by Masury. She long worked at taylor's trade, but in her widowhood has lived chiefly with her children. Died at Sam's in Ingersoll's new street.

406. Feb. 13. News of the death of Lockhart, son of Edw. Allen. Drowned, æt. 16; a son by his second wife. They have a son and two daughters by first marriage, and three sons and three daughters left by second marriage. He was with his brother-in-law Josiah Orne on his passage homeward; was lost near Cape Good Hope, 19 Oct., 1797. Named Jordan Lockhart.

407. Feb. 17. James Collins, of Robert & Sarah Hill. Suddenly, 12 months. They have seven living children, five males and two females. This was one of the twins. It was seized suddenly, as though it had swallowed something, but nothing known. It drooped, swooned, and sunk into death.

408. Feb. 17. Lydia, wife of George Lee. Consumption, æt. 24. She was a Gerry, daughter of the widow of Gen. Fisk by a former husband; one daughter left by Mr. Gerry, born in Marblehead.

409. Mar. 16. Male child of Mary Newton, alias Romiere, soon after birth. She was of the family of Newton, not of our Society. See Day Book.

410. Mar. 16. Male child of Peg Tozzer. Epilepsy, 4 years. Not of our Society. See Day Book.

411. Mar. 17. Asa, son of Asa & Margaret Dodge. Drowned, 8 years. The Captain at sea, the wife lately in this town, living at Bridge. See D. B. The child fell from the ice at Horton's Point into the North River. Two children left, a son and a daughter; born in Ipswich.

412. Apr. 2. Elizabeth, widow of Jonathan Archer. Consumption, 60. Twenty-five years married. She was a Silsbee. Archer's second wife; has two children, one male. A worthy woman. Infirm and long complaining. Her husband died last Aug., etc.

413. June 20. Robert Hill, mariner, from Lynn. Consumption, 42. Seventeen years married. She was a Collins. He has left seven children, five males and two females. Infirm for some time. Tide waiter. Poor but respected.

414. June 29. Daniel Edey, killed in Salem Harbour by lightning, 34. Two years married. He has left a wife and one male child. She a Clarke, a Gordon, alias Edey. He was killed, and one Murray, who was not of

our Society. See Day Book. Killed on board of the Martha ship, Capt. Prince.

415. June 26. Nicholas Martin, a Frenchman, Marseilles. Drowned, 22. Four years married. He has left a wife and one male child. She a Bartlett. He came young to America..

416. July 11. Debora, of Amos & Deborah Hovey. Inoculation, 5. She was a Steward, of Nova Scotia. He from Boxford. Selectman. Major. This child a twin; second left. Inoculated in Salem Hospital, 29 June, putrid spots appeared.

417. July 12. Benjamin Knights, Capt. mariner. Palsy, 60. Thirty-six years married. Left a wife; Never any children. He had long been paralytic. Inactive for six years.

418. July 16. Lyman Byrne, News of the death of. Fever abroad, 23. Grand-child of Madam Archer, etc. Parents dead. Two sisters. Died in Batavia, Java, with Capt. Jona. Hodges, mariner.

419. July 20. Sarah, of Amos & Debora Hovey. Inoculation, 22 months. This their youngest child, one daughter left. This is the second child lost by inoculation in the same class and from the same family at the Hospital. See July 11.

420. July 28. Habbaccuc Bowditch, Capt. Apoplexy, 61. Eighteen years married. He has left three sons and two daughters. His mother daughter of Col. Turner. He left a very worthy family.

421. July 30. Benjamin, of Robert & Anstis Stone. Fever, 18. They have one son and three daughters left. He was a clerk in Boston and lived at his Bro. J. Dunlap's. Died in Boston.

422. Aug. 8. Deliverance Masury, widow of Benja. Small Pox, 77. Fifteen years married. She has left two

widowed daughters. She was a White, her husband a barber.

423. Aug. 10. Thomas Lewis, mariner. Suddenly, 28. Ten months married. His wife a Burroughs, then a Dyer, one child by each, she lived with Dyer five months. He had engaged as a mariner in the U. S. Service and died as he was on foot through Lynn. He was from Guernsey.

424. Aug. 12. Elizabeth Phillips, widow of Henry. Of Fever, 51. Four years married. She was a Lambert and has left one daughter Millet. Very suddenly, supposed putrid fever; sick four days.

425. Aug. 6. Hannah Webb, alias Hannon, widow. Consumption, 40. 1st marriage seven years; 2nd marriage, 4 years. She has left five children, three males; two by Hannon, from Ireland. After very long illness, suddenly at last. She was a Murray. Both husbands lost at sea.

426. Aug. 18. Elizabeth Millet, wife of John. Fever, 25. Six years married. She has left two children, males. She was daughter of E. Phillips, who died Aug. 12. Mother and daughter were taken together. The daughter survived a week. A putrid fever.

427. Aug. 22. Francis Grant, mariner. Mortification, 66. Forty-five years married. He has left a widow. She a Smith and three widowed daughters. Dwire, alias Steward, Horton, Daniels.

428. Aug. 28. Sarah, wife of James Browne. Fever, 37. Fourteen years married. She was a Masury. Has left five children, three males. The fever was bilious, alias, etc. Her sister and three of her children are sick of the same fever. Sick eleven days.

429. Aug. 31. Samuel M., of Samuel & Priscilla Lambert. Quincy, 15 months. They have one child, a

female, left. Sick about twenty-four hours. Both parents Lamberts.

430. Aug. 31. Hannah, wife of Bradstreet Parker. Vomiting, 24. Five years married. They have two children, one male. She was born in Bradford, Mass. Seized violently, and obtained no relief, and died in forty-eight hours.

431. Sept. 6. Bradstreet Parker, merchant, fever, 28. Five years married. His wife died seven days before. He was born in Bradford, grandson to the Rev. Mr. Balch, of that place.

432. Sept. 6. Mary, wife of Joseph Hodges, fever, 37. Fifteen years married. She was an Andrew. Her mother a Gardner; four children, three females.

433. Sept. 11. Sarah, of Joseph & Mary Hodges, fever, 7. There are three children left; one son. Two sick of same fever. Mother died on 6th inst.

434. Sept 11. News of the death of Edward Cox, mariner, fever, 27. Four years married. Left a wife and had no children. His mother afterwards married an Adams and Cane. At Hispaniola upon his voyage. His wife a Gayton.

435. Sept. 20. News of Oliver Webb, captain, fever, 39. Fifteen years married. Left a wife, an Elkins, and four children, three males and one female. He was the son of William Webb. Died at Hispaniola, in August.

436. Sept. 20. John Diman Preston, captain, from Marblehead, missing, 37. 1st marriage —— years, 2nd marriage —— years, 3d marriage five years. Left a wife with two children, males. She was a widow Forbes with three children, one female; married abroad, supposed repeatedly. The Shallop sailed from Salem, 10 Nov., 1797, and has not been heard of since.

437. Sept. 20. David Mansfield, mariner, pilot, miss-

ing, æt. 52. Twenty-nine years married. Left a wife, but never had children. This man was mate, and in years.

438. Sept. 20. William Adams, mariner, missing, æt. 17. He was son of Mrs. Cox, alias Adams, Cane. This was a young seaman. The other persons did not belong to Salem.

439. Oct. 18. Elizabeth, wife of Nath. Bowditch, scrofula, æt. 19. Seven months married. She was the 2nd daughter of Capt. F. Boardman, lately deceased. There are two daughters and a son of Capt. F. B. with the widow.

440. Oct. 30. Ruth, widow of Joseph Searle. Old age, æt. 96. Forty-seven years married. Married at twenty-four. She has left two sons and two daughters, Grant and widow Chubb. Living with her younger son.

441. Oct. 31. Elizabeth, daughter of Joseph Allyne, occasioned by a fall, æt. 84. She lived a single life and for many years was a housekeeper for a Mrs. Gunter in Boston. She had a fall, after which she was never able to walk, or entirely free from pain.

442. Nov. 1. Mary, wife of Capt. Joseph Waters. Æt. 39. Sixteen years married. She has left six children, two sons.

443. Nov. 3. Rebecca, wife of Nathan Millet. Consumption, æt. 28. Four years married. She has left three children with her husband, one son. She was the pattern of Christian patience and of a most amiable disposition.

444. Nov. 8. Lydia, daughter of Samuel & Lydia Woodkind. Fever, æt. 14. She was a Lambert. He from Berkshire. This was their only child. The wife has a son by a former husband, Palfray.

445. Nov. 20. Edward, of Daniel & Bethiah Shehane.

Quincy, nine months. She was a Widger, of Marblehead. They have three children left, one son.

446. Nov. 24. Mary, of Benjamin and Mary Becket. Pleurisy, 20 months. She was a Wyman from Danvers; two children left, both males. Sick only one week; always feeble.

447. Nov. 30. Joseph Thayer, lately from Woburn. Fever, æt. 23. Two years married. He has a wife, an Edget; are both from Woburn. He came into town in June last, and she in Aug. They have one child, a female. He was a carpenter employed by Mr. Lefavre.

448. Dec. 8. Philip Furlong from Ireland, æt. 22. He came into this State in ship of Capt. T. Wellman, owned by B. Pickman, three years since; and sailed from this port. He lived not far from Waterford, Ireland. Has a mother living; died at Whitfords. Belonged to Wexford, Ireland.

449. Dec. 25. William, of John & Hannah Mack. Atrophy, æt. 3 months. They have one child left, a male. The child pined from birth and was never in health.

450. Dec. 30. Patrick Sennert, of Ireland, within two miles of Waterford, of Dunkellyn of Kilkenny. Consumption, æt. 46, He sustained a good character. As the Catholic Priest was not in town, I attended the funeral; buried 1 Jan., 1799, but he is not on my list. He came here on 9th July, 1796, in a shallop from Newfoundland, and lived first with Mr. R. Collins, then Lufkins and then removed to Mr. Ratchliffes.

DEATHS IN 1799.

451. Jan. 2. George Gilmore, of Norfolk, Virginia. W. Ind. flux., æt. 25, at the head of Pierce's wharf, Water street.

452. Jan. 4. Mary, daughter of Jonathan Archer. Consumption, 19. He has six children, three males, one daughter married.

453. Jan. 20. Benja., of Benja. & Margaret H. Bray. Quincy, 16 months. Two children left, one male.

454. Jan. 23. Anna W.yatt, died at Andover; buried in Salem. Dropsy, 33. Two children: Hannah Bray, æt. 14, and Annie Hawkins, æt. 7.

455. Jan. 30. Margaret, widow of Jacob Clarke. Asthma, 70. Fourteen years married. Married at 22. Two daughters survived her. Widow Edey and w. of Thomas Parsons. Last at Newburyport.

456. Feb. 16. Harriet, of Nathan & Rebecca Millet. Atrophy, 8 months. The mother died in Nov. last. Two female children are left with the father.

457. Feb. 24. News of the death of Benjamin Webb, at sea. Fever, æt. 23. He was a son of Joshua Webb, deceased. His mother died last year. He has a brother and three sisters. Went mate to Capt. J. Edwards, was taken, and upon his return from Guadeloupe, in Charles Derby; died 4th Feb., at sea.

458. Feb. 23. Male child of Joseph & Mary More; suddenly, in fitts, æt. 2 months. They are young, this the only child. Not of this town. He at sea. The woman apprentice at ropemaking, Vincents.

459. Feb. 23. William Thompson born in Bedford, Mass., fever, æt. 23. His mother lives in Boston and is married to Mr. Samuel Vincent. The son served as a ropemaker with Vincents. He was taken with Capt. Endicott and died in the hospital at Guadeloupe; lived at S. Silsbee's.

460. March 6. Mary, widow of Francis Grant. Cancer, æt. 75. Forty-five years married. Married at 29. Died at Robert & Mary Smith's, at the ferry, alias Beverly

bridge. Left three daughters, a brother Robert and sister widow Mehitable Patterson.

461. March 18. John Diamond, of John Diamond & Sarah Preston. Atrophy, æt. 9 months. The widow has five children with her, one female. Her husband lost at sea last year.

462. April 4. Sarah, wife of James Collins; fever, æt. 31. 1st marriage nine years; 2nd marriage, ten months. She has three living children by Evoy, one male. Collins had three children, one female. She has had one female by Collins. Her husband Evoy died abroad. Married Collins, who is in the U. S. Marine Service. She was a Richardson, father a foreigner; only child.

463. April 9. Nancy, of Jonathan & Elizabeth Palfrey. Scrofula, æt. 13 months. They have four children left, two males. She was a Vincent. He a mariner.

464. April 14. Sarah, of Joseph & Mary Brown. Fever, æt. 10 years. She was a Becket. They have four children, males.

465. April 15. Jonathan Derby, captain. Consumption, æt. 28. He was a son of Hon. Richard Derby, Esq., educated at Dummer Academy, and at Boston instructed as a merchant by his uncle E. H. Derby, and has been six voyages to India. Long sick, and confined through the winter; was at his brother Samuel's in the Mansion House.

466. April 16. Sarah, widow of John Ropes. Apoplexy, æt. 77. 1st marriage three years; 2nd marriage thirty-two years. Married at 19. She was a Titcombe, of Newbury. She married first a Stocker and then was a widow six years; then married a Ropes and then was a widow sixteen years. Left one child, married at Amherst, N. H.

467. April 22. Jean Baptiste, so called; a French

prisoner, worn out, æt. 48. He was born in Rochelle, France, from which he had been long absent in different parts of America, chiefly St. Domingo. He left a child there. He had been some time in Salem in the late war.

468. May 19. Maria, of John and Ruth Barker. Fever, 17 mo. They are a family from Pembroke, and this their only child. Have been in Salem but a few years. A blacksmith. She descended from Rev. Smith.

469. May 17. News of the death of Benjamin, son of Benj. Cloutman. Fever, æt. 16. His widow mother has many children. This a promising youth. Died 25 April in Havana, of the prevalent fever, by which we have lost many seamen. He was with E. H. Derby, jun.

470. May 17. News of the death of James, son of John Collins, sen. Fever, æt. 15. The father has left five children, out of twelve. This a lovely youth; died 5 April in Havana, of the fever there among the American ships. He was with Capt. Flint.

471. June 13. Nathaniel Osgood. Aged, æt. 88. Twenty-nine years married. Married at 34. He has left one son, Christopher. His wife was a Hannah Babbidge, married in 1745 and died Sept., 1774. He has lived with his son above twelve years. He was a distinguished shoemaker in his early life. In his temper easy. A brother now living; an old man.

472. June 20. Thomas Squires, mariner. Consumption, æt. 59. He came from Devonshire, England, æt. 19.

473. June 23. Mehitable, of Joseph and Mehitable Valpey. Dropsy in head, æt. 3 years. They have three male children.

474. June 22. Samuel, of Nath'l and Abigail Phippen. Fever abroad, æt. 17. They have one son and two daughters left. Sick in the Havanna; died on his passage, 4 June. Was with Capt. Taylor.

475. July 7. Female child of William and Mary Foye. Convulsions, 16 days. He has nine children by former wife, four males; none by the present wife.

476. July 9. News of the death of John, son of John and Elizabeth Fairfield. Fever abroad, æt. 27. Family scattered. Three daughters and four sons. Two daughters married. In the East Indies.

477. July 20. John Hodges, Captain. Hemorrheis, æt. 76. Twenty-five years married. Married at 23. A worthy man. He has left three sons and a daughter, all in reputation. Married a Manning.

478. July 27. Mary Chubb, widow, æt. 63. 1st marriage, four years; 2nd marriage, three years. Married at 20. Left no children. First husband, Edey, had children. She was a Searle.

479. Sept. 2. Male child of Daniel and Sarah Reed. 7 mos. Child born in, and parents from Danvers lately. He has one son by a former wife.

480. Sept. 3. George Cabot, of Joseph and Hannah Hosmer. 14 days. They have two daughters and a son left.

481. Sept. 15. Bethiah, of William and Sarah Millet. 15 months. This was one of their twins. They have three children. She an Archer.

482. Sept. 25. Sarah Hodges, of Daniel and Alice Ropes. 15 months. They have two children left, one male.

483. Sept. 30. Joshua, of Joshua and Lydia Webb. 20 days. A young family, first child.

484. Sept. 30. Richard Valpy. Decay, 65. Four sons and three daughters left. An honest, humble person, known as The Skipper.

485. Nov. 8. William, of William & Hannah Foster, 8 months. They have one child.

486. Nov. 10. Jonathan Mason, Sen., Capt. Apoplexy, 66. Forty-four years married. Married at 22. He has left two sons and two daughters; all have been married, many grand-children. Married a Babbidge.

487. Nov. 28. Martha Perkins, maiden. Convulsions, 43. She had lived with Mrs. Rogers from the time of marriage. She came from Ipswich.

488. Dec. 6. Elizabeth, widow of Ebenezer Whitefoot; from broken bone, 57 yrs. Nineteen years married. Married at 15. She was a Mayberry. Left two sons and four daughters.

489. Dec. 11: Lydia, of Barnabas & Lydia Herrick. Consumption, 30. Her sister died in Oct. last. No daughter left. Three sons.

490. Dec. 19. Robert, son of Pierce & Sarah Evoy. Nervous fever, 11. Father and mother both dead. Two sisters left by Evoy, one by Collins. First with a slow and then nervous fever. Sick at G. F. Richardson's.

491. Dec. 19. Eunice, daughter of Joshua & Hannah Phippen. Consumption, 20. Four sons and three daughters left.

492. Dec. 22. Andrew, son of Andrew & Hannah English. Quincy, 2 years, 8 months. One son and two daughters left.

DEATHS IN 1800.

493. Jan. 5. James Collins in the ship Constitution, mariner. Fever abroad, 41. 1st marriage, nineteen years, 2nd marriage, one year. He married at 20 a Masury and left by her three children; 2nd marriage to the widow Evoy and left one child. A man by trade a shoemaker. Two sons, one daughter by first wife, one daughter by 2nd wife.

494. Jan. 8. Abigail White, widow of Joseph White of Isle of Shoals, 78. Seven years married; married at 19. Left two children, sons. She was a Muchmore of Isle of Shoals when J. W. of Salem married her. Lived twenty years with her son Joseph.

495. Jan. 20. Male child of John & Lydia Searle. Just after birth. She was a Fairfield. Lately married. First child. She had been long very ill disposed.

496. Jan. 24. News of the death of Jonathan, son of Jonathan Mason. Fever abroad, 16. The only son by E. King, his first wife. They have two daughters by first wife and two daughters and a son by second wife. Died on board Capt. Derby at ——— in Hispaniola of yellow fever.

497. Jan. 24. News of the death of Benjamin Dorrel. Fever abroad, 19. The only son of Mrs. Strout by her former husband, Mr. Dorrel. Died on board Capt. Derby from ——— on the passage homeward.

498. Feb. 16. Anna, wife of Nicholas Lane. Rheumatic Fever, 48. Thirty-one years married; married at 17. She was daughter of Wm. Bezoill. She has left two sons and nine daughters; one son and three daughters married. Born in Cape Ann and removed to Salem after marriage. He sailmaker.

499. Feb. 20. Capt. Andrew Preston. Nervous fever, 71. Forty-six years married; married at 25. He has left one son and three daughters; two daughters married. Born in Beverly. She was a Lambert. He was an Inspector of the Customs.

500. Feb. 24. News of death of John, son of John & Hannah Collins, Sen. Fever abroad, 19. Have six children left, two males. Have lost two young sons at sea, both in the West Indies, by the Fever.

501. Feb. 24. News of death of Samuel, son of Sam-

uel & Sarah Ropes. Fever abroad, 19. Never lost a child before. They have five children left, three males. Was at Curacoa and died ashore. Sick four days. A very promising youth.

502. March 20. News of death of Philip, son of Thomas & Susanna Rue. Fever abroad and Dysentery, 22. Six children left, three sons and three daughters; one son and one daughter married. Was in the ship America from East Indies. The only person who died in the voyage of 54. Died in Dec. last.

503. April 10. Margaret, of Adam & Mercy Welman. Consumption, 19. The widow mother has one son by same marriage. She was a Mascoll and married a Stephens and then Wellman.

504. April 25. Lydia, of James & Elizabeth Archer. Convulsions, 18 months. They have four children, two males. They are both Archers.

505. June 1. Jonathan Archer. Consumption, 53. Nineteen years married; married at 24. He has left six children, three males; one daughter married. Wife died in 1791. He had lived freely. Was an assessor of the town seventeen years. A man of some information; formerly a barber. Acquired interest in the war; sold his house; was a tanner.

506. June 2. Edward Chevalier, born in the Island of Jersey. Consumption, 55. Thirty years married; married at 25. Left a wife, whom he married in Marblehead. She a widow when he married her. Came to Salem in the war from Marblehead, 1775. Had been ten years in Marblehead.

507. June 4. Susannah, relict of Jonathan Mason. Palsy and Apoplexy, 66. Forty-four years married; married at 21. Left two sons and two daughters; all have been married. Her husband died last Nov. Her

sister Ward in 1797. She was a Babbidge; her mother yet living.

508. June 7. Susannah, wife of Richard Valpy. Suddenly, 40. Nineteen years married; married at 21. Left three children, two females. She was a Backer from Marblehead.

509. July 9. Lydia, widow of Benjamin Woodman. Suddenly, 79. Thirty years married; married at 25. She was a Phillips; parents from Lynn. She had thirteen living children. A son and three married daughters left.

510. July 9. Lydia Babbidge, maiden. Fever and mortification, 67. She was the last of the children. The mother survives, aged 86. Lydia assisted the mother in a school. Madam Babbidge has kept a school above half a century. Lydia was sick about ten days. Sister of Mrs. Mason, who died in June last, and Mrs. Ward, who died Oct., 1797.

511. July 10. Elizabeth, widow of Andrew Millet. Fever and mortification, 69. Fifteen years married; married at 20. She was a Tozzer. Left two sons and a daughter. Died at her son in law Chipman.

512. July 16. Female child of Retire & Rebecca Becket. Fever, 26 months. They have one child, a male, left. She a Swasey.

513. July 31. News of the death of Tochim Jacob Rochstein. Fever, 25. Eight months married; married at 25. *She* was a natural of Gayton; married a Cox; then this husband. He was a German from Lubeck; lately came into America. Died at St. Christopher.

514. Aug. 10. News of death of Samuel, of Samuel & Anna Foot. Small pox abroad, 17. Their only son; they have three daughters. She a Crowninshield of Clifford. Died in Calcutta, on a voyage with Capt. Wheatland. Lived Essex St.

515. Aug. 17. George Archer, Capt., on his passage from Hamburg. Lost at sea, 34 years; married at 26 years. He has left a wife and four children, three females. She a Hathorne; supposed to be lost on Grand Banks in Dec. last. Lived Derby St.

516. Aug. 17. John, of John & Mary Collins, with Archer, lost at sea, age 20. They have three sons and two daughters left. A great loss in their eldest son. Turner St. They were seen so far on their passage.

517. Sept. 7. William, of Ebenezer & Sarah Slocum. Dysentery, 13 months. They have two children, one male. She a Becket. Essex St.

518. Sept. 10. Esther, of Daniel & Abigail Caldwell. Fever, 9 months. Mother a Carroll; he from Ipswich. They have three children, two males. Near Bridge.

519. Sept. 1. Fem. of Thomas & Catherine Green. Dysentery, 3 weeks. They have three children. They were from Liverpool in England.

520. Sept. 12. Male ch. of Josiah & Margaret Flag. Vomiting and purging, 12 mos. They have two females left and two males. He lately from Mason, N. H., orig. from Reading, Mass. Daniels street.

521. Sept. 13. Hannah, of Samuel & Mercy Townsend. 7 years. They have four children left, three males. She was a Stevens. Essex St.

522. Sept. 14. Nathaniel, of Nathaniel & Elizabeth Trow. 9 months. This their first and only child. She a Gilman from Newmarket. He from Beverly. Daniels St.

523. Sept. 21. News of death of James, of Thomas & Mary Hutchinson. Fever, abroad, 26 years. The widow has two sons and two daughters at home, and a son, long absent, place unknown. Turner St. He was with Mugford, at Calcutta.

524. Sept. 24. Nancy, of Jonathan & Elizabeth Palfrey. 15 months. Four children, two males, left. mother a Vincent, the youngest. Becket St.

525. Sept. 24. News of death of Joshua of widow Murray. Fever abroad, 19 years. Her only child. She was a Webb. He was with Capt. Mugford in ship Ulysses, and died in Calcutta.

526. Oct. 5. Mary, daughter of Jacob & Mary Norman. Scarlet fever, 4 years. The father dead. The mother an Archer, she married a Gunnison, then Norman, now Peters. One child left by Gunnison. Essex street.

527. Oct. 16. Abigail, widow of Zachariah Curtis. Aged, 86 years. Married at 20; seven years married. She was daughter of John Gray. Turner, between Essex and Derby.

528. Oct. 20. Lois, widow of Samuel Odell. Consumption, 55 years. Married at 22; she died in Pleasant st. Has left four sons and three daughters. She was a Larrabee of Lynn. Her husband died in 1790.

529. Dec. 12. Male child of Lydia, daughter of Daniel Cloutman. 2 years.

530. Dec. 28. News of the death of Capt. Elisha Harrington, drowned, 35 years. Married at 28 years. She a Burrill; her second husband. Three children left, one son. He from Weston. He was cast away on George's; crew were saved; were in a brig from Jamaica.

531. Dec. 28. News of the death of John, son of Johnson & Ruth Briggs. Fever, 19 years. The widow has six children left, three sons and three daughters. Left by Capt. John Fairfield at Havanna.

532. Dec. 28. Capt. Adam Wellman missing, lost at sea. 27 years. Married at 26 years. He married Nancy, the eldest daughter of widow Browne. No chil-

dren. Son of Adam Wellman, who died abroad in 1786. They sailed for Ireland 10th Jan. from Salem, and on 5th of Feb. from New York.

533. Dec. 28. John Crandall, mate with Capt. W. Putnam, missing. 41 years. Married at 32 years. He married the eldest daughter of Nicholas Lane and had three children, one male. He was from Providence, R. I. Sailed 12th Feb. for Gibraltar.

534. Dec. 28. James Carroll, with Capt. Putnam, mariner, missing. 19 years. The only son of James Carroll, who married a Webb. Seven daughters left.

535. Dec. 28. John Cloutman, mariner, 2d mate with A. Wellman, missing, æt. 23 years. Son of Joseph; his mother a Becket. She has one son and three daughters left.

536. Dec. 28. Thomas Stephens, boy with Capt. A. Wellman, missing. 14 years. The widow has three daughters left. Her husband was lost in 1784.

DEATHS IN 1801.

537. Jan. 22. Mary, of William and Anna Foster. Worms, 4 years 4 months. They have another child. She a Knapp. Essex Street between Turner and Becket.

538. Jan. 30. William, of William and Anna Foster. Throat distemper, 4 months. They have no other child, have lost three.

539. Jan. 30. Margaret, daughter of Joseph and Margaret Strout. 10 months. Their only daughter, they have 4 sons. Essex Street between Herbert and Curtis. Father a Lieut. in the American Navy.

540. Feb. 3. Sarah Burroughs, child of Daniel Geering. Fever, 20 years. Her mother a Stillman.

541. Feb. 4. News of the death of Jacob Whitte-

more. Fever, 23 years. 2 sons and daughter left with the mother Mary. At Martinico.

542. Feb. 6. John, son of Maj. Gen. John Fiske. 21 years. Only two sisters are left, married to Allen and Putnam. Essex Street between Beckford and Dean.

543. Feb. 13. Mary, wife of Christopher Beals. Bilious Fever, 33 years. One year married. She was a Bacon of Lexington. The second wife of her husband. Two children, one by each wife, males. They had lived but a little time in Salem. He from Boston, a ship-joiner. Essex Street, corner of Turner.

544. Feb. 21, Sarah, widow of Capt. Oliver Webb. Fever, 35 years. Married at 17 years, and time in marriage 15 years. She was an Elkins. Her husband died 1798. Three sons and a daughter left. Born E. part of Salem. Essex Street, corner of Turner.

545. Feb. 27. Elizabeth Manning, maiden. Complication, 72 years. There are two brothers and two sisters living together, rich and unmarried. Essex Street between Herbert and Curtis.

546. March 3. Sarah, wife of Robert Smith, aged 80. Married at 18 years, a Gatchell, with whom she lived 12 years. Has lived with Smith 43 years, and leaves one child, who married a Phillips of Marblehead. Her maiden name was Knights. She lived in her native town, Marblehead, till the war. Mr. Smith's second wife lived near Essex Bridge. Smith is a fisherman, and had children by his other wife.

547. March 13. Judith, dau. of George and Judith Archer. Scarlet fever and throat distemper, 5 years. He was lost at sea last year. The widow was dau. of Daniel Hathorne; has had three children, one male. The child sick three weeks. Resided in Winter Street.

548. March 20. Hannah, wife of Emmons Smith.

Consumption, 51 years. Married at 22. She a dau. of Thomas Dimon. Four sons and three daughters left. Resides on neck, below Ingersolls.

549. March 21. Hannah, wife of Joshua Phippen. Consumption, 60 years. Married at 23. She was a Sibly and left four sons and three daughters. Was very active in early life, long sick and confined. Resides Hardy, below Derby Street. He a cooper.

550. April 11. William Scott, son of Thomas and Mary Ashbey. Atrophy, 15 months. She was a White. They have four children, one son. Resides Essex Street, between Orange and Curtis. He a Captain.

551. May 8. Moses Stickney, of Brentwood, N. H. Drowned, 25. Has no relations in this town in which he has lived about two years. He was born at Newburyport and educated at Brentwood. He was assisting to load a sloop with rocks, and in a high wind attempting to get from the neck to the sloop was drowned. See D. B.

552. June 6. Female child of Michael and Mary Bateman. Convulsions, 6 days. She was a Batten, four children, one male. He a foreigner, mariner. Child taken suddenly. Resides Turner Street, between Derby and Essex.

553. June 29. Mary, widow of Henry Chipman from Newburyport. Aged 84. Married at 18. First marriage sixteen years. Second marriage thirty-four years. She was a Carr; married a Nowell and lived at Newburyport, then a Chipman; left two sons and three daughters. She had lived above a year in the family of her son-in-law, Joseph Vincent, and died under the natural infirmity of age. Born in Newbury.

554. July 8. Lydia, widow of Abraham Valpy. 66 years. Married in 1756, at 20; 18 years married. She was a Clough. Her father from Boston. One daughter

survived her. Born in Salem near the windmill. Resides in Daniels Street. He a fisherman.

555. July 24. Mary Foot, dau. of William and Rebecca Oliver. Canker on Bowels, 3 weeks. They have three children, two sons. She a Whitford. Resides in Webb Street. He a soapboiler.

556. July 25. Sarah, widow of George Dean. Consumption, 28 years. Married at 18 years, and 8 months married. She was a Phippen, and left one child, a male. Resides in Hardy Street, below Derby. Long sick. Lost a sister and mother within two years, by Consumption.

557. Aug. 4. Benjamin, son of Samuel and Sarah Ropes. By accident, 19 years. Mother a Chever, have six children, left three sons. A worthy youth. First interment in the new ground in Brown Street. He was helping to lower the fore top-mast of the ship Bellisaurus, at Union Wharf, and was crushed between the two at the cap; death instant. See D. B.

558. Aug. 5. Hannah, wife of James Perkins, yellow fever, 26 years. Married at 24. Was a Porter, born in Nova Scotia. Left one child, a female. Essex Street, corner of Hardy. He a blacksmith. See D. B.

559. Aug. 16. Stephen, child of William and Hannah Webb. Obstructed breathing, 2 years 9 months. She was an Allen of Marblehead. They have four children, two sons. Resides Hardy Street, between Essex and Derby. He a mariner.

560. Sept. 2. George Underwood, son of John and Hannah Macewen. Vomiting, 8 months. She was a Townsend of Salem. He from Scotland, three children left, two sons. They have lived at Kennebunk.

561. Sept. 7. Female child of Joseph and Sarah Traske. Atrophy Infantile, 18 months. She was a

Dodge, both from Beverly. A young couple. He a blockmaker. Resides Daniel Street, below Derby.

562. Sept. 13. Micah, son of Nathaniel and Deborah Kinsman. Dysentery, 1 year 7 months. She was a Webb and lived formerly at the Fort. Two sons left. Resides Essex Street, opposite East. He a Captain.

563. Sept. 18. Elizabeth Stone, dau. of Gamaliel and Sarah Hodges. Dysentery, 2 years 8 months. She was a Williams, four children, three sons left. Resides Essex Street, between Orange and Daniel. He a Captain.

564. Sept. 24. Elizabeth, of Jeremiah and Susanna Abbott. Dysentery, 10 months. He was from Andover last May. She a Center, from Charlestown, Mass. One daughter. Living below Ash Street, on the bank of North River. He a truckman.

565. Sept. 25. Elizabeth, dau. of John and Nancy Pierce. Dysentery, 10 months. She was a Sibly; her father from England, her mother from Beverly. Two daughters left. Living in Turner Street below Derby. He a blacksmith.

566. Sept. 26. Judith, wife of Joseph Miller. Consumption, 23 years. Married at 20. Her father was Deacon Kinsman of Gloucester, and her *father's* father, Col. Warner of Gloucester. They have lived in Salem two years. He was from Gloucester. Ropemaker and painter. Two daughters left. Resides on Brown Street on the common. She born in Gloucester.

567. Sept. 29. Hannah, wife of John Collins. Dropsy in the head, 52 years. Married at 20. She has left five of her own children, two sons; one dau. lives of his first marriage, besides two daus. married Batchelder and Chever. She was a Porter, born in Littleton. Her parents removed from Wenham. She lived long in Danvers. He a fisherman and lived with his former wife six years.

568. Sept. 30. Judith, dau. of Joseph and Judith Miller. Atrop. Infant, 10 months; youngest child.

569. Oct. 1. Mary, dau. of John and Mary Berry. Fever, 15 months, only dau. They have three sons. She was a Ward. He a Captain. Resides Essex Street, corner Turner.

570. Sept. 28. Robert, son of Robert and Hannah Bartlet. Dysentery, 2 years. She was a Tarbox; by marriage a Stanley. Has five children by Stanley and one by Bartlet. Resides Liberty Street, between Vine and Water. He a mariner.

571. Oct. 4. Emmons Smith. Fever, suddenly; 54, married at 25. His wife a Dimon; died in March last. Four sons and three daughters left. He was born in Ipswich.

572. Oct. 5. Miriam, wife of John Lewis. Dysentery, 52 years. Married at 51 years. She was a Maley of Marblehead; lived in Fort Gerry, then with son Fiske, then Jacob Crowninshield. Upon death of her sister married sister's husband, removed five months since to Salem. Resides Brown Street, on Common. He of Newburyport, ropemaker; has seven children.

573. Oct. 4. Nathaniel, son of William and Elizabeth Hampson. Dysentery, 13 months 16 days. From Marblehead, ropemaker. He has lived in Salem eleven years. She an Eliot from Marblehead. Four children left, one daughter. Daniels Street.

574. Oct. 5. Edward, of Daniel and Bethiah Shehane. Dysentery and fever, 18 months. His father from Isle of Wight. She a Widger from Marblehead. Three children left, one son. Mariner. Becket Street.

575. Oct. 5. Joseph, son of Joseph and Mercy Webb. Dysentery, 2 years and 3 months. She was a Devereux of Marblehead. He a boat-builder. Left two daughters. Becket Street.

576. Oct. 8. Elizabeth, dau. of Edward and Elizabeth Archer. Fever, 2 years and 6 months. She was a Phippen, one son left. He a ropemaker, child long sick. Bridge Street, opposite Locust Street.

577. Oct. 9. Edward, son of above. Fever and dysentery, 1 year. No child left.

578. Oct. 8. Lydia, dau. of Joseph and Lydia Walden. Fever, 1 year and 8 months. She was a Flint from Lynnfield. He from Danvers. Four sons left. He a ropemaker. Pleasant Street.

579. Oct. 10. W. Browne, son of Samuel and Nancy Masury. Fever and dysentery, 1 year. She a Browne. Four children left, two sons. Captain, mariner. Charter Street, corner Fish.

580. Oct. 11. Lemuel Winchester, of Andover. Dysentery, 36 years. Married at 24. He has four children, two sons by his wife, who had two children by a former marriage. He came to work the season in town as a carpenter, leaving his family in Andover, came with *her* daughter. Bridge Street, opposite Locust, same house with E. Archer.

581. Oct. 12. Sarah, dau. of Joseph and Mary Browne. Fever and dysentery, 1 year and 7 months. She was a Becket. They have four sons left. Captain, mariner. Essex Street, opposite Pleasant.

582. Oct. 13. John, son of Mary Gardiner. Dysentery, 4 years. She was a Collins; married Simon Gardiner. Three children left by him, two sons. Essex Street, corner of Herbert.

583. Oct. 14. Patty, daughter of Joshua and Ester French. Dysentery, 3 years and 6 months. She was a Butman. They have four children left, three daughters. He a truckman. Lives Flint Street, between Essex and Chestnut.

584. Oct. 15. Lydia, daughter of Joseph and Mary

Peele. Dysentery, 1 year and 3 months. She was a Lufkin, one son left. Derby Street, near Blaney Street. He a mariner, absent.

585. Oct. 16. Samuel, son of Samuel and Susanna Caban. Dysentery, 1 year and 2 months. She was a Ruee. His father came in early life from France. Their only child. Becket Street. He a mariner, absent.

586. Oct. 19. Mary, dau. of Moses and Lydia Townsend. Dysentery, 8 years and 6 months. They have four children left, one son. She was a Lambert. He a captain of a ship. Derby Street, below Turner.

587. Oct. 20. George, son of John and Lydia Albree. Chin cough, 1 year and 4 months. He from Medford and his wife also. She from the ancient family of Tufts. Lived in Salem several years, then left and returned two years since. He a trader. Two children left, one son. Daniels Street between Essex and Derby.

588. Oct. 29. James, son of James and Mary Clearage. Fever and dysentery, 8 years. He was from Kittery, Maine. She a Foote, of Salem. He married 15 years ago, and afterward removed to Newfield, 90 miles. He has lately returned to Salem. Five children, one male. He a ship carpenter and caulker.

589. Nov. 3. Mary, dau. of William and Elizabeth Carlton. Cough and dysentery, 9 months. A twin child, two daughters left. She a Cooke. He a printer.

590. Nov. 7. Susanna, dau. of Ebed and Deborah Stoddard. Cough and fever, 13 months. She a Marsh from Hingham. He from Hingham, a shoemaker. Six children left, one son. Derby Street, near corner of Daniels.

591. Nov. 12. Margaret, wife of Charles Johnson. Fever, 27 years; married at 26. She a Whitefoot. He from Gothenburg in Sweden. One child, a son. Williams Street.

592. Nov. 15. Patience, wife of Richard Nichols. Fever, 39 years, married at 19. First marriage one year. Second marriage sixteen years. She was a Collins; first married a T. Stevely; four children, one son, one dau. by Stevely included. Broad Street, west end.

593. Nov. 22. Male child of John and Elizabeth Bonnemaison. Convulsions, 9 months. He came from Martinico, and married at Salem, 20 Aug., 1794, then removed to Martinico. She daughter of Rev. Johnson. She at Salem on a visit, Court Street. He a merchant.

594. Nov. 30. Male child of Ester White. Hooping cough, 9 months. Her grandfather a Masury. Her mother married a Burke.

595. Dec. 5. Eunice, widow of William Cooper. Consumption, 48 years; married at 22, married 8 years. She was a Swasey. He an Englishman; 18 years absent, where, unknown; left no children.

596. Dec. 7. News of the death of William, son of John and Elizabeth Reath. Fever, abroad, 23 years. He was born on Salem plains, but lived till lately at Marblehead. His parents have not lately lived in Salem. He died at sea. Mate with his brother John.

597. Dec. 8. Mary, widow of Asa Whittemore. Consumption, 52 years. Married at 17; 27 years married. She was a Potter from Beverly, born at Chebacco, Ipswich. He was from Danvers. He died at Boylston. Left two sons and one daughter. Mrs. Whittemore's father killed by Ellingwood, of Beverly. Always feeble. A good mother. Husband a mariner. At first a blacksmith.

598. Dec. 13. Notice of the death of John, son of Samuel and Mary Knapp. Fever abroad, 40 years. Married at 18 years. First marriage seventeen years. Second marriage, three years. He was born in Ports-

mouth. His first wife a Gavett of Salem; left three daughters. His second wife a Dodd of Salem, has one son. He was on his passage from Batavia to Philadelphia, in the Brig Harriet, Capt. Isaac Hagar.

599. Dec. 13. Ester, wife of Joshua French. Debility, 40 years; married at 22. She was a Butman, left four children, three daughters. From Wenham. Flint Street.

600. Dec. 13. Mary, wife of Thomas Ashby. Debility, 36 years; married at 26. His second wife, she was a White. He lived but a short time with the first wife. Three daus. and one son. Essex Street between Curtis and Orange.

601. Dec. 16. Capt. John Baton, of Isle of Oleron. Rupture, 72 years; married at 21. He was a Huguenot from Rochelle. He came early [in 1745, see D. B.] to Salem and married a widow Lander, who was a Slade. Four daughters survived him. He was of good character, much esteemed and respected. Long infirm but not confined. English Street, below Derby.

602. Dec. 17. Ruth, widow of Capt. Johnson Briggs. Fever, 46 years; married at 17, married 22 years. She has left six sons and three daughters. He died abroad in 1794. She was a Stileman. Union St.

603. Joshua, son of Joshua and Ester French. Fever abroad 14 years. The mother and another child have died this year at home. He was at Batavia with Devereux when he died.

604. Capt. Samuel Townsend. At sea, 39 years; married at 28. He has left a wife and five children, two sons. He sailed from Salem and has not been heard of. She a Stevens.

605. Samuel son of Samuel and Elizabeth Masury. At sea, 19 years. The mother a Webb. He was with Capt. Townsend.

606. James, son of James and Hannah Collins. At sea, 19 years. Parents dead. He was with Capt. Townsend.

607. William; son of William and Elizabeth Fairfield. At sea, 17 years. His mother a Becket. He was with Capt. Townsend.

608. Richard, son of Richard and Mary Collins. Fever abroad, 26 years. His mother a Cox. Two daughters left. A mariner, had been three years absent; died at Philadelphia.

DEATHS IN 1802.

609. Jan. 2. Edward, son of James and Hannah Murray. Fever, 2 years. The mother a Cox. Two children left. Curtis Street.

610. Jan. 3. Susannah Welden, a maiden. Palsy, 84 years. Her parents came from Scituate before her birth. She has lived thirty years in Danvers. She had been paralytic before the last shock. Her mother's name Elizabeth.

611. Jan. 3. Mary Ann Richardson. Lung fever, 90 years; married at 20, married 51 years. She had ten sons and two daughters. One son and one daughter survived her. She was a Dupy of Boston. Lived in Salem nine years with her daughter Sweetzer. Her husband David Richardson, of Woburn. Her son blind by accident, living in Woburn. Derby St. near Daniels.

612. Jan. 4. Deborah, wife of James Becket. Palsy, 42 years, married at 23. Left four daughters and two sons. She was a Peabody from Haverhill. This was the second stroke, the other six months before. Her mother a paralytic. Becket Street, below Derby.

613. Jan. 29. Mary, widow of William Cox. Pleurisy fever, 67 years, married at 27, married three years.

She was a Village. Left one daughter, widow Macdaniel. See D. B.

614. Feb. 12. Nicholas, son of Nicholas and Elizabeth Martin. Convulsions, 3 years. She was a Bartlett. The husband was drowned several years since, one son, John, left. Daniels Street.

615. Feb. 20. Female child of William and Elizabeth Cody. Quincy, æt. 10. The mother a Welcome. A son left. She married a Williams and Jeans since.

616. March 7. A child of James and Hannah Murray. Fever, æt. 10. One child left, they buried one in January last. The mother lays sick. Curtis Street.

617. March 19. William Sage from Connecticut. Consumption, æt. 53. Married at 33 years. He was from Middletown, Conn. He left one child, a son. His wife a Welcome, has two children by Smith. Webb St.

618. March 27. John, son of John and Priscilla Clark. Atrophy, 20 years. Father and mother long time dead. Only one surviving sister, Priscilla. Curtis Street.

619. April 2. Thomas Palfrey. Scrofula, 33 years, married at 25. Left three children. He was a son of Warwich P., formerly a Dept. of the Customs of Salem, by a second wife, who was a widow Bickford, a Ward. He married widow Gale, who was a Crowninshield. His father left him an estate of great value. He was an active man. She had children by Gale and three sons by Palfrey. Derby Street, near Daniels Street.

620. April 7. Hannah, wife of James Murray. Consumption, 33, married at 20. Left one child, a dau. Her husband has not been heard of for several years. She was a Keen, and has lost two children this year. Curtis Street.

621. April 18. Reuben, son of Reuben and Catharine

Shad. Dropsy in head, 7 years. She has been long a widow. Two children left, one son. She a Coffrin. Derby, corner of Daniels Street.

622. May 12. Elizabeth, of Jona. and Sarah Browne. Fever. 21 years. Her mother a Twiss. She addressed by B. Waters. They have two sons and a daughter left. Taken Saturday of malignant scarlet fever, and died Wednesday morning. Lived on Allen's farm on the Neck.

623. May 28. Hannah, daughter of Daniel and Deborah Sage. Fever, 5 years. She was daughter of S. Silsbee. He from Scotland and at sea. A son and daughter left. Daniels Street.

624. May 29. Daniel, brother of Hannah, last named. Fever, 3 years. (See 1795, three children lost by same fever.) Sick 41 hours only.

625. May 29. Mary, widow of John Ward. Fever, 51 years, married at 18 years. Lived with her first husband, an Emerton, 7 years, and with her second husband, Ward, 5 years. He died Dec., 1789. She a Lufkin from Ipswich. Had son and daughter by first marriage. Daughter married Luke Heard.

626. May 30. Sarah, wife of George Sinclair, of consumption, 25 years; married at 23 years. One child, a son left. She was a Mascoll, married in 1799. Her husband a foreigner and absent. Complaining 9 months, removed during her sickness to her mothers. Derby Street, between Carlton and Becket Streets.

627. May 31. George, son of Sarah Sinclair, above. Fever, 9 months; buried in same coffin with its mother.

628. June 5. News of the death of Samuel Rantoul. Abroad, 21 years. His mother a Preston. Father died abroad. A brother and sister living. His father from England, worthy, died in 1782. He had been an apothecary in Salem and his health directed a voyage, and he

died of consumption in Bilboa, 20 April. With Capt. Haskell, of Beverly.

629. June 14. Olive, wife of Isaac Perkins. Fever, 35 years, married at 23. She was a Phippen. No child. She was seized violently with scarlet fever on Monday; sick seven days, had been complaining. On Derby Street near Neck.

630. June 22. Hannah, one of the twins of William and Elizabeth Carlton. Fever, 18 months. One child, a female, left. The other twin died in November last. She a Cooke. Essex between Newbury and Union Streets.

631. June 26. Mary, of James and Mary Stocker. Measles and consumption, 5 years. The father has one female child left. His wife (a Herrick) died a few years since. Child under care of grandparents. County Street, near Ash.

632. July 1. Charles, of Charles and Margaret Johnson. Fever after measles, 1 year. The mother died in Nov. last. The father at sea. A Frenchman.

633. July 8. Susanna, of Susanna Preston. Consumption, 17 years. The mother a daughter of Capt. Andrew Preston. His wife a Lambert. Sick a year, confined six months. Essex, opposite Pleasant Street.

634. July 8. Capt. Thomas Dean. Mortification, 79 years, married at 28 years; lived one year with first wife and forty-one with second wife. Leaves one dau. by each wife. He was son of Capt. Thomas Dean and leaves a brother and two sisters. Derby Street. See D. B.

635. July 12. Lois, wife of Andrew Cole, of Beverly. Consumption, 33 years, married at 30. She was a daughter of John and Elizabeth Fairfield. Lived much in Beverly and married there. Long sick; came over to her parents and died while on her visit. Only child died. Turner Street between Essex and Derby Streets.

636. July 30. Deborah, of Daniel and Deborah Sage. Dysentery, 19 months. One son left, absent with his father in the East Indies.

637. July 31. George, of William and Patty Boyd. Atrophy inf., 3 months. He from Ireland, she a Franks. Two children left, one male.

638. July 31. News of the death abroad of John Gray, of fever, 31 years, married at 23. Left three children, one daughter. He a son of John Baton, and a worthy man; married a Browne. Died mate of a ship at Batavia. Barton Court.

639. Aug. 16. Elizabeth, of George and Hannah Hodges. 7 months. Their youngest child. She a Phippen. He has two children, one son by former marriage and one daughter left by the present. Hardy Street, below Derby.

640. Aug. 17. Mehitable, of John and Miriam Perkins. Complication, 29 years. The parents from Topsfield, 1785. She a Smith. They have four sons left, two by a former marriage; moved to farm on Neck, then to last house on Derby Street, near Neck.

641. Aug. 18. Hiram, of Nathaniel and Eunice Shed. 2 years and 3 months. The parents lately from Amherst, N. H. Three children, one daughter. She a Fairfield, of Amherst. Derby Street, between Daniels and Hardy, on Palfrey's land.

642. Aug. 24. Mary, wife of Luke Heard. Dropsy, 33 years, married at 21. She was an Emerton. Her mother died in May last, and had married a Ward; one child, a son, left. Heard from Lancaster. He had been for many years infirm. Derby Street, between Daniels and Hardy Streets.

643. Aug. 24. Elizabeth, wife of Capt. John Edwards. Dropsy, 56 years, married at 24. She a dau. of Rev. Samuel Fiske, of Salem, and he a foreigner.

She has left a son who married a Browne and a daughter who married a Street. She had long been infirm. See D. B. Essex Street above Elm.

644. Aug. 28. Susanna, widow of John Hathorne. Aged 80 years, married at 25 years. Her husband died after three years of marriage. She was a Tousel, and descended from the ancient families of English and Hollingworth. Col. Hathorne is her son. Daughter married an Ingersoll. See D. B.

645. Aug. 15. Stephen Shehane, killed by lightning at sea, 22 years. There is a widowed mother and three sons, two married. Benjamin married and one child; Daniel married, four children, one son. He was in the Belisarius. See D. B. Several were injured, he only was killed.

646. Aug. 28. News of the death of William Becket. Scurvy, at sea, 30 years, married at 26. He has left a widow (a Waters) and one son and one daughter. The mothers of both, widows. He sailed with Capt. Felt from Isle of France, and they both died on the passage. W. Becket died 2 July last.

647. Sept. 8. Jonathan Twisse, farmer on the Neck. Palsy, 69 years, married at 23 years. One child left. He came from Danvers upon the Neck farm, then Ives' farm, and lived there twenty-eight years. His only child married a Browne and lives on the farm. He was a large, strong man and very honest and esteemed.

648. Sept. 10. Mehitable, widow of Capt. William Paterson. Dysentery, 60 years, married at 27 years; lived with husband twenty-four years. She was a Smith; the family lived near ferry. Her husband dead nine years. Left four children, one daughter married a Byrne. She was complaining, confined ten days. Her eldest son married. In Herbert Street.

649. Sept. 11. Sarah, widow of George Underwood. Dysentery, 67 years, married at 20. She was a Lambert. Married Matthew Butman, of Beverly, 1755, lived with him nine years; married John Underwood 1768, and lived with him eight years. A child John and a son by Underwood, George, left. Her second husband died abroad. The collateral branches of family numerous. Essex Street, corner of Becket.

650. Sept. 14. Ezra Trask from Beverly. Dysentery, 79 years. Married at 23 and lived fifty years with first wife, Joannah (Green), who died 1797, aged 81 years. He took his 2d woman before Dr. Putnam, of Danvers, in 1801, and she died soon. He had lived in Danvers and not long in Salem.

651. Sept. 15. Eunice, of Nathaniel and Eunice Richardson. Consumption, 23 years. She was their only daughter. They have four sons. She was addressed by a S. Hunt, of Charlestown, N. H. Father from Woburn, mother from Danvers, a Putnam. East Street.

652. Sept. 19. Joseph Lambert, of Moses and Lydia Townsend. Dysentery, 16 months. They have three daughters left. The father at sea; she a Lambert. Derby, corner of Carlton.

653. Sept. 21. Amelia, daughter of William and Sara Patterson. Atrophy Inf., 23 months. They have four children left, two sons. She an Archer, daughter of John. Walnut Street.

654. Sept. 24. Thomas, son of William and Hanna Webb. Dysentery, 16 months. They buried one child thirteen months ago. They have three left, one son. She an Allen of Marblehead. Hardy Street.

655. Sept. 30. Susanna, of Andrew and Hanna English. Dysentery, 3 years. They have three children left, one son, all sick. She a Patten. Williams Street.

656. Oct. 10. John, of James and Elizabeth Archer.

Atroph Inf., 17 months. They have four children left, two sons. She an Archer. Essex St., corner of Pleasant.

657. Oct. 3. John Andrew, of Rev. Nathaniel and Mary Stone. Dysentery, 7 months. She an Andrew, on a visit from Windham. Their only child. Winter St.

658. Oct. 10. Olive, wife of Zechariah Marston. Dysentery, 38 years, married at 33 years. She a Shelden, of Danvers. Two children, one son. He had also two children by a former wife. Essex St., corner of Union.

659. Oct. 11. John, of Zechariah and Olive Marston. Dysentery, 1 year.

660. Oct. 11. Hannah, wife of Andrew English. Dropsy, 36 years; married at 21. She a Patten. Three children, one son.

661. Oct. 12. Mary, wife of John Williams. Dysentery, 46 years; married at 26. She a Webb. Three children, one son. A daughter has married a Victory and a Rind. He born in London. Becket Street. Infirm for a long time.

662. Oct. 13. Mary, daughter of John and Elizabeth Emerton. Fever, 3 years. She a Bartlett from Marblehead farms. He from Chebacco. Three children left, one son. Turner Street below Derby.

663. Oct. 14. Charles, of John and Sarah Babbidge. Dysentery, 15 mos. She a Becket. Six children living, three sons. Essex Street, near Union.

664. Oct. [*]. [*] s of Joseph and Lydia Walden. Dysentery, 8 mos. They have four children, all sons. He a ropemaker, industrious. She a Flint from Lynnfield. Baptized in 1801. Long sick and the mother and children. Pleasant Street.

665. Oct. 21. Isaac Perkins. Dysentery, 88 years, married at 25 years; 1st marriage, forty-one years, 2nd

---

*MSS. mutilated.

sixteen years. Left widow and four children, three sons in town, dau. widow Woods. See D. B. All came from Topsfield into the town of Salem. Derby, Neck Gate.

666. Oct. 23. Samuel, of Samuel and Abigail Webb. Atrophy Inf., 10 years. Son of John Webb, she a Palfrey, two children, females. Hardy Street below Derby.

667. Oct. 28. Thomas Mascoll. Dysentery, 64 yrs. Has two sisters, widow Mary Welman and the widow of Pasca Foot, called Tammy. Derby, corner of Becket.

668. Nov. 28. John Hubbard, of John and Martha Fairfield. Scarlet fever and throat distemper. 3 years. They have two daughters left. She a Hubbard of Ipswich Hamlet. He a son of Dr. W. Fairfield of Wenham.

669. Dec. 13. Priscilla Lambert, of Matthias and Hannah Rice. Scarlet fever and throat distemper, 4 years. She was a Lambert of Salem and married M. Rice, a physician, of Saco, and removed to Blackpoint, Me. He died several years ago. Left three males, child born at Scarborough, widow removed to Salem last year.

670. Dec. 14. Female child of Henry and Sarah Prince, at birth. He was from Ipswich. She a Millet. They have six children, two males.

671. Dec. 15. Thomas, of Thomas and Mehitable Rue. Scarlet fever and throat distemper, 3 years. She an Archer. One male child. Her mother Kimball, past 80, and his mother's mother, a Becket, past 70, at the funeral. Essex, corner of Turner Street.

672. Dec. 17. Richard Goss, of Bradford. Apoplexy, 53 years, married at 27 years. 1st marriage, one year; 2nd, sixteen years; 3rd, four years. Leaves five children. He born in Bradford, a ship carpenter. Third wife a Eulen. His surviving children by second wife.

673. Missing. Capt. Hardy Millet. Lost at sea, 25 years, son of John Millet. Full name was Joseph Hardy.

DEATHS IN 1803.

674. Jan. 2. Elizabeth, wife of William Daniels. Asthma, 42 years. Married at 20 years. She was a Grant at the ferry. He a boat builder from Hingham. Leaves two sons and four daus.

675. Jan. 8. Nicholas Lane, of Thomas and Charlotte Magoun. Scarlet fever and throat distemper, 8 months. Their first and only child. She a Lane. He from Pembroke, a ship carpenter. Carlton Street.

676. Jan. 8. Adeline, of Samuel and Susanna Archer. Fever, 5 months. She was a Babbidge. He son of Samuel. Six children, two males. Walnut Street.

677. Mar. 5. William, of Zachariah and Olive Marston. Fever, 4 years. The mother and another child died last October of dysentery. St. Peter Street below the church towards the river.

678. Mar. 6. Abijah, of Abijah and Mary Hitchins. Fever, four years. She was a Cloutman, her mother a Becket. His mother a Gardiner. Carlton Street.

679. Mar. 25. Mary Smith. Consumption, 27 years old. She was a granddaughter of Thomas Diman, an honest news carrier.

680. Mar. 28. Nathaniel, son of Nathaniel and Mary Hitchins. Fever, 14 months. She was a Webb. One female child left. Bottom of Turner Street.

681. Apr. 1. News of the death of John Rogers at sea. 26 years old. Married at 23 years. He married Eliz. Foot, a Crowninshield. He was born in Ipswich in England. One son left. He died on his passage from Canton to Boston, of fever.

682. Apr. 1. News of the death of Edward, son of Edward and Hannah Stanley. Shipwrecked, 17 years of age. Born in Salem. Father dead and mother married R. Bartlett. Shipwrecked in Virginia and perished.

683. Apr. 1. Concluded that Sam. Molloy is dead. Aged 25 years. Married at 22. One son left. Married Nancy Foote, a Crowninshield. Born in Salem and has been missing three years.

684. Apr. 10. News of the death of Ebenezer Tozzer, of Fever, abroad. 46 years old. Married at 38. He was a son of Mrs. Whitefoot, who died at 103. His wife a Patterson. Two daughters left. Born in Salem. On his passage from Gaudeloupe in the Brig Trial, 25th March.

685. Apr. 10. News of the death of James Crelly. Fever, 42 years old. Married at 27. He was from Ireland. She a Valpy. Five children, four females. Sick six days, died 18 March with Capt. Ober.

686. Apr. 10. News of the death of Stephen Waters, son of Benjamin and Lucia Waters. Dysentery, 19 years old. Father of Salem, mother a Dane of Ipswich, sister of Hon. Nathan Dane. A brother and two sisters left. Parents dead. Died soon after he left Calcutta, in a ship commanded by Joseph Orne of Salem.

687. Apr. 13. Mary, dau. of Mansfield and Joanna Burrill. Consumption, 25 years old. He from Lynn in early life. She a Silsbee. They have two sons and three daughters left.

688. Apr. 22. Martha, wife of James Whittemore. 34 years old, married at 21. A Clemens, born in Salem.

689. Apr. 21. William, of William and Hannah Webb. Convulsions and worms, 6 years of age. She an Allen. They have left four sons and two daughters.

690. Apr. 25. Hannah, wife of Robert Bartlett. Fever, 45 years old. Married at 19 years. 1st marriage 14 years; 2d marriage 7 years. She was a Tarbox of Lynn, married a Stanley and afterwards a Bartlett. By Bartlett a son. Two sons and one daughter by Stanley living.

691. Apr. 29. Margaret Manning, of Benjamin and Hannah Hodges. Consumption, 12 years of age. They have four daughters and a son left. Mother a King.

692. June 15. Hannah Hodges, widow of N. Archer. Age, 86 years old. Married at 19 years. Daughter of Gamaliel Hodges (see Day Book), and married an Ives and Archer. Lived many years a widow. No children survived her, but G. G. children.

693. July 27. Capt. Edward Allen, sen'r. Obstruction in intest. canal, 68 years old. Married at 24 years. In first marriage fifteen years, in second twenty-five years. He married Ruth Gardner, alias Hodges, 18 Jan., 1759. He married Mary Lockart of N. C., 1778. Left a son and two daughters by first wife and three sons and three daughters by second wife. See Day Book.

694. Sept. 2. Charlotte, of Joseph and Mary Waters. Vomiting and purging, 10 years old. Mother a Dean, died Nov., 1798. Four daughters and two sons now left.

695. Sept. 2. John Loring, of John and Ruth Barker. Teething, 12 months. She granddaughter of Rev. Smith. Both from Pembroke. Two daughters left. A few years in Salem. Blacksmith.

696. Sept. 2. News of the death of Amos Hill, of West-India fever, 23 years of age. Married at 22. He was from Richmond, Va., not long in Salem, mar. Elizabeth, daughter of Rob't Bartlett. One daughter left. Died in Gaudeloupe, 22 July.

697. Sept. 14. Josiah Warren, of Josiah and Elizabeth Gatchel. Atrop. Inf., 14 months. They have one son left. She a daughter of Nich. Lane. He from Brunswick, Me. Ship carpenter.

698. Sept. 15. Female child of Nathaniel and Mary Silsbee. Injury at birth, two days old. She was a daugh-

ter of George Crowninshield. He was a son of Nath. Silsbee. Merchant.

699. Sept. 27. Wm. Cooke. Taylor, etc. Apoplexy, sd by Jury. 51 years old. Married at 22. First marriage ten years, second marriage nineteen years. He has left a second wife, and two children by first wife a son and daughter. Daughter married a Becket. Wife a Brown, widow Rankin. First wife a Marston. He was from Cambridge. See Day Book.

700. Sept. 28. Sarah, wife of Benjamin French. Consumption, 35 years old. Married at 26 years. She a granddaughter of Rev. Emerson of Topsfield, named Emerson, and has lived in and near Boston. No children. He a carter. Essex Street, near Flint Street.

701. Oct. 1. Joseph J., son of Joseph Jenkins and Abigail Knap. Dysentery, 10 months. She a Phippen, one daughter left. Derby, corner of Herbert Street. Captain, mariner.

702. Oct. 7. Mehitable Smith, of William and Sara Patterson. Inflammation of Bowels, 18 months. She an Archer. Three children, two males. Herbert Street. Captain, mariner.

703. Oct. 13. Edey, wife of Henry Stanley. Fever, 28 years old. Married at 24 years. She was a Picket of Beverly. They have two children, females. Her first husband left a child. He had a wife at Lynn, married two years. Liberty below Charter, mariner.

704. Oct. 13. Jonathan, of Benjamin and Elizabeth Cloutman. Scarlet Fever and throat distemper, 12 years. She was a Fry. The father died 1797. Four daughters two sons left. Webb Street. Father was a carpenter.

705. Oct. 23. Thomas Benson, of Robert and Hanna Peele. Fever, 10 mos. She a Benson. Four children left, two males. Carlton Street. Father a mariner.

706. Oct. 23. Mary, of Benjamin and Mary Millet. Scarlet fever and throat distemper, 7 years. She a daughter of Wm. Peele. G. mother a Becket. Essex, corner of Herbert Street. Father mariner.

707. Oct. 24. Mary, wife of Benjamin Macdonald. 42 years old. Married at 30 years; a Cox, born in Salem. He from Ireland, died in the Amer. ship Essex. Two daughters.

708. Oct. 29. William, of Nath. and Hannah Western. Scarlet fever, etc., 6 years. The mother a Richardson from Woburn. Have seven children left, one son. Carlton Street. Father a shoemaker.

709. Oct. 29. Lois, of same. Same disease, 3 years. Father from Reading.

710. Oct. 31. Samuel, of Mansfield and Sarah Burrill. Quincy, 7 months. She a Randall of Isle of Shoals. Four children, two sons. Federal Street. Father a carpenter.

711. Nov. 3. Henry, of Joseph and Marg. Strout. Quincy, 7 years. She a Battoon, widow Dorrell. Three sons left, one by first husband. Essex, corner of Curtis. He a Lieut. in the Am. Navy.

712. Nov. 16. Margaret, wid. of W. White. Relax. of Bowels, 74 years of age. Married at 23, married life not quite a year. She was a Lambert and lived many years a widow. A good and agreeable temper. Much esteemed. Her husband was an Englishman, a mariner. She lived Essex, corner of East Street.

713. Nov. 19. John Bray, a venerable man. Of gradual infirmity. 80 years old, married at 24 years, and had a married life of 28 years. His wife a Driver, long dead. Two sons, dau. married B. Webb, one son married. His parents died aged. He was long infirm. A man of the greatest industry and most peaceful temper. Essex, opposite Herbert. A shoemaker.

714. Nov. 19. Martha, of John and Eliza. Hill. Quincy, 2 years. She a Browne. Six children, four sons. Charter, corner of Fish Street.

715. Nov. 23. Sarah, of Nath. and Sarah McIntire. Nervous fever, 7 years. She a Sheldon. Both from Reading. Three children, two daughters. Have been in Salem five years. A laborer for Mr. Fogg. Daniel Street below Derby.

716. Nov. 29. Nancy, of James and Hannah Carroll. Quincy, 6 years. She a Webb, dau. of John. Six daughters left. Carlton Street.

717. Nov. 30. Mary Adelaide, of Benjamin and Mary Babbidge. Nervous fever, 3 years. She a daughter of Joshua Phippen. They have one son left. Essex, between Herbert and Union Streets.

718. Dec. 14. Samuel Silsbee, Sen. Pleuritic fever, 73 years old. Married at 26 years. His wife a Prince. Left one son and two daughters, married to Daniel Sage and David Patten. Essex, corner Daniel Street. Quite a healthy man, not very active.

DEATHS IN 1804.

719. Jan. 8. Eunice, dau. of William and Ruth Prat. Quincy, 5 months. He from Weymouth. She from Braintree. A Wills. Five children, three sons. Not long in town. Webb Street.

720. Jan. 9. James Tytler from Scotland. Perished on the Neck in a violent rain storm. 58 years. Married in Scotland, æt. 24 years. Thrice married. Has lived on Salem Neck since he came to America in Aug., 1795. He has a wife and two daughters, all in Salem, came with him. He had two wives and children behind. See D. B.

721. Jan. 5. Rose, negro servant of widow St. Webb. Deformed, palsy, 31 years of age.

722. Jan. 20. News of death of Capt. Enoch Swett. Fever at sea, December 21. 37 years of age. Married at 32 to Nancy Williams. No children. He was born in Newburyport.

723. Jan. 27. Penn, twin child of Samuel and Mary Townsend. Quincy, 4 years and 7 months. He was lost at sea. She a Welman. Other twin named Moses. Four children left, three sons. Essex Street, opposite Pleasant.

724. Jan. 31. Martha, widow of Christopher Babbidge. Mortification, 62 years of age. Married at 19. First marriage not one year, second marriage twenty-four years. She was a daughter of Silsbee of Salem. Married first an Emerton in 1761, then Babbidge. Left four children, two sons.

725. Feb. 8. George Wade, son of George and Abigail Newell. Fever, 16 mos. One child, son, left. He from Kennebeck, Bowdoin. She from Ipswich, a March See D. B.

726. Mar. 6. Samuel Bishop. Tide waiter in Customs. Convulsions, 44 years. Married at 28, sixteen years in marriage. He was from Marblehead. He had been in the Revenue Boat since its establishment. His wife a Cox of Salem. Four children, one son.

727. Mar. 20. Barbara, wife of Samuel Tibbets. Consumption, 37 years of age. Married at 19. First marriage fourteen years, second marriage two years. She of Danvers. He a mason from New York state. No children left. Both of German descent. She was long sick, but looked fresh. She a Bullock, grandmother an Ulmar. First husband a Goodhue. Essex, corner Hardy Street.

728. Mar. 25. Benjamin, of Henry and Sara Prince. Atrophy Inf., 1 month. She a Millet. He from Ipswich.

They have three sons and two daus. left. Mother very infirm. Derby Street, between Daniel and Orange.

729. Mar. 28. Col. Samuel Carlton. Palsy, aged 73 years. Married at 23 years of age. She a Eunice Hunt of Salem. Left two sons and five daus.; two married, Mrs. Barr and Mrs. Helmes. He was with the army in 1778 returned, was sick and paralytic, much enfeebled, and confined fifteen years. Union Street.

730. Apr. 11. Jonathan,.of Jonathan Archer. Running sores, aged 20 years. She was Rachel Woodman. They have ten children left, three males. First child's death in the family. The first child I ever christened. Lame many years.

731. Apr. 11. Benjamin, of Benjamin Hodges. Consumption, aged 19 years. She a Hanna King. Four daus. left. He graduated at Cambridge last year.

732. Apr. 24. Asa, of Timothy and Lydia Tibbets. Convulsions, 2 years of age. She was a Browne from Ipswich. He from Albany. One child left, a son.

733. June 3. Susanna Babbidge, schoolmistress. Fever, 90 years old. Married at 17 years; 12 years in marriage. She was a Becket and had seven children, four sons, three daus., and has many of her posterity. See D. B. She was removed from her home on Essex street, while it was repaired; immediately taken sick and died at Archer's. Walnut Street.

734. June 15. Male child of Jonathan and Ester Smith. 24 hours after birth. They were both from Lynnfield. She a Smith, cousins. Her mother a Hart. Came to Salem in 1803. Two children living, one male.

735. June 17. Female child of George and Abigail Newell. 6 hours after birth. See Feb. 28 of the present year.

736. July 13. James Carroll. Consumption, 55

years old. Married at 23 years, and 22 years in married life. He was born in Berwick, Maine. Married Hannah, dau. of John Webb. He lived till lately on the River, bottom of Daniel Street. Died in Carlton Street.

737. July 15. Capt. Samuel Ingersoll. Fever at sea, 60 years of age. Married at 28 years. He married Susanna Hathorne at Hampton, 19 Oct., 1772. Left a son and dau. His son survived him one week.

738. July 22. Capt. Ebenezer, son of above. Fever, 23 years of age. On board same ship with his father and died at the Quarantine ground, Salem.

739. Aug. 13. Anna, widow of Adam Welman. Consumption, 30 years of age. Married at 25, one year in marriage. She was a dau. of Nath'l and A. Browne. Her husband died abroad. She was addressed by a son of Capt. B. West at the time of her death.

740. Aug. 19. Capt. John Becket (military). Paralytic, 58 years of age. Married at 23. First marriage five years, second marriage fifteen years, third marriage thirteen years. Descended from ancient family of Becket. Two sons and four daus. First wife a Browne, second an Ingersoll, third a Dean. An active, social, benevolent man. Sick about three years. Shipwright. Becket Street. See D. B.

741. Aug. 19. Male child of Benj. and Mary Silver. 9 months. She a Bullock, dau. from the Ulmer family. Corner of Hardy and Essex Streets, opposite meeting house.

742. Aug. 21. Male child of Margaret Crispin. Atrophy Inf., 5 months. The mother a dau. of Wm. and Margery Crispin and granddaughter of widow Mary Tazell. Crispin from England.

743. Aug. 21. George Ellison, mariner. Obstructions in int., 32 years old. Married at 28. Father an

Englishman, mother an Ulmer. The mother's family from Germany. George married a Foster of Ipswich, one son. See D. B.

744. Aug. 25. Bethia, dau. of John and Rachel Archer. Mortification, 12 years old. Nine children left.

745. Aug. 25. Female child of Wm. and Hannah Cordwell. 9 months. She was a Hitchborn. They removed from Boston to Maine several years ago, and lately to Salem. Five children, three sons. Bridge Street.

746. Aug. 31. Mary Lee, of Samuel and Priscilla Lambert. Quincy, 14 months. They have a son and dau. left. He at sea. Both Lamberts, of Joseph and Jonathan. Court Street.

747. Sept. 19. Male child, of Joseph and Martha Webb. Convulsions, 8 days old. She a Devereux of Marblehead. Three children left, one son. Becket St.

748. Sept. 20. Alexander, of Alexander and Elizabeth Donaldson. 8 mos. She a Peele. One child, a dau., left. He from Ireland, blockmaker. Becket St.

749. Sept. 16. News of the drowning of Alexander Allen, at sea. 26 years. He was a twin child of Edward and Mary Allen. The widow has three children of Capt. Allen's by a former wife, and five of her own, two sons, other one son. He fell from a yard that broke on his passage homeward.

750. Sept. 23. Capt. Nathan Millet. Fever, ague, etc., 32 years. Married at 24. Four years in marriage. Son of Jonathan and Sarah. Left two daus. Mother died in 1798. He had lately returned from W. Ind., sick. Corner of Essex and Herbert Streets.

751. Sept. 28. Female child of Thomas and Mary Goldsmith. Atrophy Inf., 9 mos. She was a Whitford. Goldsmith her second husband. Her former husband a Hill. Four children by both marriages, two sons, two daus. Derby Street, corner Webb Street.

752. Sept. 30. Male child of Thomas and Sarah Webb, at birth. She was a Kilby from Hingham. They have one child, a female, left. Derby Street below English and Webb.

753. Oct. 2. Mary, wife of Thomas Goldsmith. Nervous fever, 41 years. Married at 21. First marriage five years, second marriage five years. She was a dau. of John and Mary Whitford, married Hill in 1784; he died in 1789. She married second, Goldsmith, in 1799. She has left three children by first marriage, one son, and one by last marriage, a son.

754. Oct. 3. Elizabeth, widow of Capt. John Batôn. Suddenly, 79 years. Married at 19. First marriage three years, second marriage fifty-one years. She was a Slate. She married Jona. Lander 1745, and John Batôn in 1750. Batôn died Dec., 1801. She had ten children. Died suddenly, without complaining, in her chair. Her two sons by Lander are dead. Four daus. by Batôn survive. English Street below Derby.

755. Oct. 14. Charles Cooke, of William and Elizabeth Carlton. Fever, 14 months. They have one child left, a dau. Essex Street, below Union and Walnut.

756. Oct. 22. John Perkins. Debility, 60 years. Married at 25. First marriage sixteen years, second marriage eighteen years. He was from Topsfield in 1785 and lived ten years on Derby's, afterwards Allen's, farm, at the Neck. First wife a Heard from Topsfield. Second a Merriam from Boxford. Four sons, two by each marriage.

757. Oct. 23. Capt. Jona. Millet. Scurvy, 41 years. Married at 25. He was a brother to Nathan, who died Sept. 23. His wife a Masury. Left six children, five sons. He returned on 21st from Batavia and had been mate under his brother-in-law Ropes. Hardy Street between Essex and Derby.

758. Oct. 26. Stephen Cloutman. Consumption, 49 years. Married at 26. His wife Hannah Smith. Ten children, six males. He from one of the old Salem families. Ship carpenter, graver and caulker. Webb Street on Collin's Cove side.

759. Nov. 11. Hannah Weston. Consumption, 20 years. The father, Nath'l, from Reading, shoemaker; mother Hannah Richardson, of Woburn. They have now five daus., two sons. Long sick. Addressed by Abraham Knowlton. Carlton Street.

760. Nov. 12. Mary Stevens. Consumption, 21 years. Dau. of late Capt. Thomas Stevens; his wife a Valpey, who has two daus. Mary lived with her grandmother Welman. Hardy Street, between Essex and Derby.

761. Dec. 16. Mary Chever, maiden. Paralytic, 80 years. Descended from an ancient family. Nursed long in Judge Lynde's family. Died at Capt. Timothy Welman's, a cousin. She possessed a house in Essex Street, opposite Orange Street. Lived two years with Welman. Derby Street, west of Hardy Street. 80 in August last.

762. Dec. 29. Capt. Thomas Ashby. Debility, 41 years. Married at 24 years. First marriage one year, second ten years, third two years. Descended from an ancient family. First wife unknown. Second wife Mary White, died in March, 1791, four children. Third wife an Ashby, married March 13, 1803, one child; in all five children, one son, four daus. Essex Street, corner of Curtis.

763. Dec. 30. Mary, dau. of James and H. Carroll. Atrophy, 7 years. She was a Webb. The father died in July last. Five daus. left. Carlton Street.

DEATHS IN 1805.

764. Jan. 31. Jesse Kenny. Convulsions, 41 years. He came from Middleton. Married, at 29, Hannah Mascoll. Two children left, a son and daughter. He a tanner.

765. Feb. 1. Male child of Greenleaf and Elizabeth Porter. At birth. He from Haverhill and she from Danvers. Liberty, below Charter street.

766. Feb. 6. Robert, of Robert and Hannah Pecle. Fever, 6 years. Great distress in the head, but no delirium. She was a Benson. Three children left. One son. Carlton street.

767. Feb. 16. Samuel Jefferds. Apoplexy, 27 years. Married at 19 years. Left three children, one son. She was a Green of Marblehead; he from Boston, a brass-founder. Essex, opposite Curtis street.

768. Feb. 17. Richard Nichols, baker. Consumption, 40 years. Was always feeble. He married, at 21, Patience Collins, who died Nov., 1801. He was from Rhode Island. Left three children, one son.

769. Feb. 22. Male child of Benjamin and Elizabeth Hutchinson. Fever, 18 months. She was a Hitchins of Marblehead. Five sons left. Turner, below Derby street.

770. Mar. 24. Thomas Welcome at Guadeloupe. Fever, 22 years. Son of T. W. by a Lambert. Both parents dec'd. Two own sisters left. A promising young man. Mate with Capt. Penn Townsend of the brig Edwin. Educated by Moses Townsend.

771. Mar. 24. Richard Furber at Guadeloupe. Fever, 18 years. An orphan child. His mother a Chever. One sister. Educated by his mother's sister. Bapt. 19 Nov., 1786. Much esteemed. Was with T. Welcome in the brig Edwin. P. T. Master at Guadeloupe.

772. Apr. 4. Capt. Samuel Masury. Fever, 40 years. Married, at 28, Nancy dau. of W. Browne. They have five children, two sons. Below Pleasant street, north of Common, in New street.

773. Apr. 11. Josiah Gatchel, a carpenter. Cramp in stomach, 28 years. Married, at 23, Sarah Lane dau. of Nicholas Lane. He from Brunswick, Me., and his parents, etc., are still living. Long confined by cramps and rheumatism. Two children left, males. Corner of English, on Derby street.

774. Apr. 14. Phœbe, wife of William Browne. Consumption, atrop., 63 years. Born in Danvers, came from Andover; her father from Jersey. She a Ganson, and married first a Porter, second a Carlton, third a Browne. First marriage at 26. Time of first marriage, 14 years; second, 3 years; third, 19 years. She brought a niece with her, Phœbe Buxton, from Andover. Mrs. Browne has two sons and seven daughters; six have been married. Curtis street.

775. May 5. Joseph Searle. Worn out, 79 years. He was a true child of nature, with no education, no regular calling. His father a butcher. He married, at 24 years of age, first, Martha Dean and lived with her twenty-six years. He married second, Margaret Becket, she being sixty years old, and lived with her eleven years, and she died in 1789. No children. Lived formerly in the Becket House, near shore.

776. July 19. Benjamin Hutchinson. Suddenly, 37 years. His father was a blacksmith, as he also was, at head of Long Wharf. He married, at 23, a Hitchins from Marblehead, and lived with her fourteen years. Five children, all sons. Turner, below Essex street.

777. July 21. Elizabeth, dau. of James and Sarah

Chever, consumption, 18 years. Her mother a Brown. They have three sons and three daughters living. The eldest daughter married a Cook. Essex, opp. East street.

778. July 24. William Carlton, a printer. Infl. fever, 34 years. Son of William. Had been indisposed ever since his imprisonment for printing a libel upon T. Pickering. Died in the highest state of derangement. Married at 23, and lived nine years in marriage. His wife was a Cooke, her mother a Stone. His mother a Palfrey. One female child. See D. B. Essex, near Union street.

779. Aug. 9. James Shehane, son of Daniel. Yellow fever, 18 years. Died in Jamaica, taken by English. Was with Capt. Bullock. His mother Sarah Masury. Two sons left.

780. Aug. 25. Elizabeth, widow of William Carlton. Consumption, 34 years. Of scrofulous habit, of long confinement. She was a daughter of Charles Cooke. Mother a Stone. Brought up by an aunt, wife of Capt. Joseph White. Born within a few days of her husband. At Capt. White's, cor. St. Peter's and Essex streets.

781. Aug. 26. Mary Ann, of Benjamin and Nancy Kittridge. Dysentery, 21 months. Sick three weeks. Father practises physic. They came from Brookfield and New Bedford. No children left. East, cor. of Pleasant street.

782. Sept. 7. William, of John and Hannah McEwen. Atroph. inf., 15 months. He from Scotland, she a Townsend. They have four children left, one daughter.

783. Sept. 7. Sarah, wife of Capt. William Patterson. Consumption, 38 years. She married at 26, and was a daughter of John Archer. Prospects great in early life. Four children left, one daughter. Herbert street.

784. Sept. 20. Bethia, dau. of William and Sarah

Millet. Dysentery, 2 years 3 months. She an Archer. Five children left, one son. Essex, cor. of Pleasant street.

785. Sept. 26. Female child of William and Mary Crispin. Dysentery, 20 months. She a Dawson. Nine children left, one son. Winter street, east side near Hay Market.

786. Sept. 27. News of death of Capt. Nathaniel Browne, son of Nathaniel. Fever at sea, 34 years. He died on the 9th of June, fifteen days out, after seven days illness, on his return from Batavia in the ship Recovery. His mother was a Meservey. He married, at 26, Mary Pickering of Salem. A most worthy man. Three children left, one son. Daniels street, Elwyn's Point.

787. Oct. 7. John Archer of William and Sarah Patterson. Atroph. inf., 2 months. She was an Archer and died last month. Three children left, two sons. The father once of good prospects. Child in care of James Archer and buried from his house. Essex, cor. of Pleasant street.

788. Oct. 13. Lewis, son of John and Jane Stickney. Bowels disorder, 18 months. The parents and children came from Newbury. He came as shipwright and has been a few months in Salem. Seven children, one daughter. Webb street, near the neck.

789. Nov. 1. Susanna, wife of Thomas Rhue. Fever, etc., 58 years. Married at 18 years of age, and time in marriage 40 years. A daughter of W. Becket. Had been faltering through the summer, sudden at last. Five children left, two sons. Derby street, cor. of Daniels.

790. Nov. 12. Samuel Brooks, merchant. Nerv. fever, 47 years. Fever continued twenty-three days. Moved into Salem from Woburn. Married at 33, a Gill.

They have five children. He has many brethren. He was a most amiable man. Neptune, cor. of Elm street.

791. Nov. 26. News of the death of Capt. David Patten, drowned at sea, on the passage in a sch. with freight from Trinidad to Baltimore. Thrown by the motion of the vessel suddenly from the deck, and sunk immediately, aged 38 years, having been married but two years. He was of Salem, left an orphan. Educated by S. Silsbee, whose youngest daughter he married. No children.

792. Nov. 28. Male child of Daniel and Mary Kenny. Atroph. inf., 3 months. Never well from birth. He was from Middleton, Mass. She was a Hill. They have five children, two sons. Derby street, between English and Webb.

DEATHS IN 1806.

793. Feb. 7. Female child of Peter and Hannah Clifford. Atrop. inf., 8 months. Only child. He from Dorchester, N. H. She from Salisbury, Mass. Family, Edwards. They have been in Salem a few months. Turner street, between Essex and Derby.

794. Feb. 10. Female child of Henry and Joanna Webb. Fever, 8 months. The grandparents of the child, all four, living in health. She a Burrill, both of Salem. Three children left, all females. He a son of John Webb. The collateral branches numerous. Essex street, opposite Curtis.

795. Feb. 13. Priscilla, dau. of William and Mary Allen. Scrofula, 10 years. He from Manchester, Mass., married first, Hannah Edwards, who died leaving three daughters, this the second. The second wife, a Hunt. The first wife from Manchester, dead four years. Hardy street below Derby.

796. Feb. 16. Joseph English. Fever, aged 72 years. He has one brother Philip, who is sexton of the East Meeting House. His father John came from Isle of Jersey, young, by invitation of P. English. Lived in the eastern part of the town, and was employed while at home by the heirs of Philip English, who was grand uncle to his father.

797. Feb. 17. James Collins, son of William and Mary Foye. Worms, 5 years. The mother was dau. of James Collins of Salem, and widow of Ledbetter, by whom she has two daughters, Andrews and Foye. Essex street, below East, near Neck Gate, so called.

798. Mar. 4. James Philips, a native of Great Britain. Killed, aged 30 years. Came from Wales. He married, nine months previous to his death, a Peabody from Andover. No children. He was discharging cannon on Crowninshield's wharf, and by some strange omission neglected to sponge. Daniels street.

799. Mar. 21. Female child of William and Rebecca Wing. Atroph. inf., 6 weeks. He from Plymouth. She a Saunders, from Marblehead. Lately came to Salem, Two daughters. Derby street, between Carlton and Becket.

800. Apr. 13. Capt. Benjamin Hodges, a man of great worth. Consumption, 52 years. He married, at 24, Hannah King of Salem, and has left four children, daughters. They have buried five children of consumption. Essex street, cor. of Orange.

801. Apr. 18. Nancy, of Edward and Margaret Allen, 22 years. Father died in 1803. Was from Berwick-on-Tweed. Mother a Lockhart, from North Carolina. See D. B. 19, 1015. Mother, two sons and two daughters left. At Andover.

802. Apr. 21. Cuffaloe, a black man from Boston,

Consumption, 50 years. Twice married, first at thirty years of age and second at forty years. Lived fifteen years with his first wife, and nine with second, who was born in Plymouth county, free. He had a wife in Barbadoes. Nine years in Salem. Collins street on Shallop Cove.

803. Apr. 24. Robert Smith, died at his daughter's in Marblehead. Aged, 82 years. He was descended from Smith at the ferry, an ancient family. Married twice; first, at 23 years, a Hollet, of Marblehead, by whom he had two children, one son and one daughter. His second wife was a Knight, by marriage a Gatchel, by whom he had one daughter. First marriage, 5 years; second marriage, 43 years. A few years ago, the mansion house was sold and repaired, and he lived among his children. Not a year between his first and second marriages.

804. May 11. Mary, widow of Charles Collins. Fever, 39 years. She was a Munyon, married at 17, and left five children, three sons and two daughters. Eldest son at sea, mate of a vessel. Husband died Nov. 9, 1800. Brown street, near Washington Square.

805. May 15. Elizabeth, widow of John Gray. Fever, 33 years. Husband died in 1802. She was a Browne, married at 21. Left two sons and an infirm daughter. Not long sick. English street.

806. May 19. William Newman, a black man from Providence. Worn out, 20 years. Came to Salem a mariner. Was taken sick and carried to the Charity House where he died in a few days. Lethargic while there. Has a mother living in Providence, R. I.

807. May 20. Female child of Emmons and Mary Smith. Atroph. inf., 5 months. She was a Gowing of Danvers. Two children left, both females. On the path below Webb street, towards Shallop Cove.

808. May 23. Anna, widow of Benjamin Gale. Palsy, etc., 82 years. She was a Philpot and second wife to B. G. whom she married at 50 years of age; lived 11 years in marriage. One child is left by a former wife and three families of grandchildren. Essex, corner of Pleasant street.

809. June 7. Cornelius Bartlet. Convulsions, 32 years. His wife Grace Bowden from Marblehead. He from Plymouth, Mass., of four children. One daughter. He was a tanner with Capt. Collins, traded at sea. Married at 20, and time in marriage, 12 years. Derby street, near Becket.

810. June 12. Emmons Smith. Consumption, 28 years. A ropemaker, industrious and of good habits. Long confined. Married, at 21, Mary McGowen of Danvers. He of Salem. Two daughters. Buried a child May 20. Webb street near Shallop Cove.

811. July 6. Mary, widow of Benjamin Waters. Consumption, 74 years. She a Dean. Twice married. First at 20 years of age, George Ropes, who died soon; time in marriage two years. Second, at 26, Benjamin Waters, with whom she lived 27 years. Her second husband lost at sea. Long a widow, insensibly declining for long time. Brother and sister left. Has left two daughters, one is the widow of William Becket with two daughters. Children by Waters. Vine street.

812. July 10. Benjamin French. Convulsions, 37 years. Twice married; first at 22 years, lived 10 years in marriage; second at 35. First wife from Maine. Second wife Elizabeth Beckford of Salem. He from Woburn. Truckman. Three days sick. One child, male. Hardy street, between Essex and Derby.

813. July 13. Henry Webb, a mariner, son of John

Webb. Convulsions, 35 years. Sick only three days. Married, at 25, a Burrill of Salem. Three children, females. Essex street near Orange.

814. July 24. Mary, of Retire and Rebecca Becket. Convulsions, 5 years. The child complained on Monday morning and died on Monday night. She was a Swasey. Two children left, a son and daughter. Derby street, near Becket's wharf.

815. Aug. 16. Samuel Oakes, shipwright. Nervous fever, 17 years. He was from Cohasset, living with a brother in Carlton street, at a trade with him. Sick one week, last three days senseless. Of good reputation.

816. Aug. 19. Abigail, wife of John Watson. Debility, 54 years. She was a daughter of Capt. John White, and married at 18. She has been long failing. A most kind neighbor. Left three sons and two daughters. One son married in Portland; a daughter Parker in Salem.

817. Aug. 20. News of death of Capt. Daniel Archer. Consumption, 30 years. He was a son of Jona. Archer, and had been five years from home. Died at Liverpool in England, June 3rd, lingering. Was master of a ship for Mr. Murray, American Consul. Two brothers and three sisters left.

818. Sept. 7. Raymond, son of John and Elizabeth Emerton. Atroph. inf., 9 weeks. Child feeble from birth and small. He from Chebacco, Ipswich. She, a second wife, a Bartlet from Marblehead. Four children, two males. Lane below Derby street, between English and Becket streets going to the water.

819. Sept. 26. Benjamin Gale, son of Benjamin. Nervous fever, 21 years. He had been a clerk to his uncle Clifford. Father died in the infancy of the son.

Wife Martha Crowninshield. Only child by Gale. Now widow Palfrey. Has children by Palfrey, males. Derby street between Daniels and Orange.

820. Oct. 1. Margaret, widow of George Lazell. Asthma, 74 years. She was a Swasey. Married a W. Crispin, in 1755, and then Mr. G. Lazell. First marriage, 12 years; second, 17 years. One child, a son, by Crispin. Her mother Swasey now living aged one hundred years. Her only brother Samuel aged 76. Daniels street.

821. Oct. 6. News of the death of Capt. Eliphalet S. Patterson. Fever abroad, 25 years. Died at sea, Aug. 18. He was a son of one of my best friends, Capt. W. Patterson. Eliphalet Smith a name from his mother's family. He has two brothers, and a sister married W. Byrne.

822. Oct. 7. Male child of Antony and Mary Silver. Fever, 14 days. He from Portugal, second husband. She a granddaughter of Mr. Mc'Rhue, of Neutral French. A Longeway. First husband a Pascal. Derby street, corner of Turner.

823. Oct. 12. Sarah, dau. of Nathaniel and Abigail Phippen. Nerv. fever, 21 years. Just ready to marry a Mr. Oakes, brother of Samuel who died in August last. Mother a Hooper, both of Salem. He a son of Deacon Phippen of the Society. Two children left, one son, and daughter who married a Knapp. Essex street, above Newbury and Elm streets.

824. Oct. 25. Josiah Choate. Nerv. fever, 27 years. Was a shoemaker, and then kept a retailer's shop on the Long Wharf. Much esteemed and prosperous. Sick many days. He was from Chebacco, and at 23, married a Hutchinson. One child, a female. Curtis street.

825. Nov. 2. Capt. William Patterson. Convulsions, 36 years. His father one of the best of men. His wife an Archer, whom he married at 24, and she died last year. He was confined about two days. Left two sons and a daughter. Herbert street.

826. Nov. 2. Widow Dorothy Williams. Consumption, 74 years. Married at 19, and had nine children. Lived fifteen years in marriage. She was lately from Marblehead. Lived with her granddaughter Davis. Very infirm a long time. Left a son and daughter. Essex, between Union and Walnut streets.

827. Nov. 6. Female child of Elizabeth Collins. Atrophy, 9 weeks. Hardy, between Essex and Derby streets.

828. Nov. 25. Samuel, son of Samuel and Margaret Bishop. Nervous fever, 10 years. Sick three weeks. Father died Mar. 6, 1804. Mother a Cox. An only son. Three daughters left. Carlton street.

829. Nov. 28. Female child of Timothy and Sarah Welman. Convulsions, 3 days. Well at birth. She an only daughter of the late Capt. Silsbee. One child left. Derby, near Hardy street.

DEATHS IN 1807.

830. Jan. 4. News of the death of Henry Rice. Drowned at sea, 22 years. He was in his duty upon the rigging and fell from the jib. From East Indies bound homeward. His father, Matthias Rice, was a physician in Saco and its neighborhood. She a daughter of Capt. Joseph Lambert of Salem.

831. Jan. 25. News of the death of Samuel Thomas. Drowned at sea, 22 years. He was upon duty, and fell

from the mast. From West Indies bound for Wilmington, N. C. His father, Capt. William Thomas, absent. His mother Elizabeth. She a Stileman. Three children left, one son.

832. Feb. 13. Peter Murray, a cooper. Consumption, 61 years. Long enfeebled. Married, at 25, a daughter of Stephen Webb, with whom he lived twenty-four years. She died in 1795. He left only one child, a daughter, who married Israel Ward, a barber. Becket street.

833. Apr. 10. Capt. John Edwards. Paralysis, 64 years. He was infirm for a long time and not paralytic, but in the last stages of his sickness. He was born on the Rappahannock, Va., came early to Salem, and married, at 24, a daughter of Rev. Samuel Fiske, Elizabeth, sister of the late Gen. John Fiske, with whom he lived thirty-four years. Left two children, a son Capt. John Edwards, English street, and a daughter who married Thomas Street.

834. Apr. 24. Anstis, dau. of Robert and Anstis Stone. Consumption, 29 years. A woman of sterling worth. The mother a Babbidge by Anstis Crowninshield. One son and two daughters left. One the widow Dunlap. Hardy street.

835. May 14. Sarah, widow of Daniel Shehane. Paralytic, etc., 63 years. She was a daughter of Benjamin Masury, married at 23, and lived twenty-seven years with her husband who came from Ireland. Two sons left, married. Essex street, near Neck gate.

836. May 17. Miriam, widow of John Perkins. Fever, 52 years. Was sick but eight days. She was a Smith from Boxford, married at 31 years, and lived eighteen years with her husband who died in 1804. He had

two children by a former wife, and two by this, living now. Derby street near Neck gate. Had lived on Derby's Neck farm.

837. May 23. Sarah, wife of Abijah Hitchins. Paralysis of the brain, 52 years. See D. B. She a daughter of B. Gardner, ropemaker, married at 20. From Boston at marriage, and he from Lynn. Five children, two married. Twenty-eight years in Salem. Becket street.

838. June 4. News of the death of Capt. George Ropes. Drowned at sea, 43 years. He was in the Gulf of Gibraltar, and was washed overboard in the evening. He married, at 22, a Seth Millet. Left four daughters, three sons and two children deaf and dumb. For the account, see D. B., June 5. Becket street.

839. July 17. Capt. Jonathan Beckford. Missing, 37 years. Born Aug. 7, 1770. He sailed from Surinam and left for home early in March, and has not yet been heard from. A flourishing man of good habits, son of Jonathan and grandson of late deacon Beckford. He married, at 24, a daughter of Samuel Chever. Has left one daughter, who is the only child. Curtis street.

840. July 22. Margaret Swasey, born Feb. 14, 1707. Aged, 100 years. She was a Diamond of Marblehead, and married, at 23 years of age, S. Swasey, of Salem. Four years in marriage. Cheerful, temperate and industrious. See D. B. Had two children, one son who survives, aged 77. Daniels street, oldest house in Salem.

841. Aug. 2. Capt. Thomas Williams. Delirium and atrophy, 38 years. He was brought from England at seven years of age by Capt. F. Boardman. He married first, at nineteen, a widow Symmes who was a Swasey; second, in 1794, a Smith; and third, in 1796, a widow Cotton who was a Babbidge. Returned from

West Indies. See D. B. Aug. 4. Had left two children, one by first and one by second wife. Hardy street.

842. Aug. 9. News of the death of Michael Barnes. Fever abroad, 27 years. A son of Major Barnes. Was on his passage, as second mate, from Surinam, with Capt. Searle, who also died. He married, at 24, Eunice, dau. of W. Peale. Left two children, males. Becket street.

843. Sept. 5. Male child of Lewis and Sarah Eustis. Atrop. inf., day after birth. He a truckman, from N. H. She a Martin from Boston. Second child. None living. They lived in the old Pickering house. Essex street, between Union and Walnut.

844. Sept. 7. Richard Graves of Maryland. W. In. flux, 26 years. He was from the low countries, a mariner, into Salem. Died in the Charity House. Long sick.

845. Sept. 13. John Black, a worthy African. Fever, 65 years. Brought to Salem by Capt. Foster.

846. Oct. 7. Capt. Robert Richardson. Dysentery, 73 years. A foreigner from England. Married 1st at 33 years, in 1768, Sarah Nurse, and lived sixteen years with her; and 2nd, in 1793, widow Hunt, living with her fourteen years. Died at Barnstable. Left two grandchildren from first stock. He a pilot. Hardy street.

847. Oct. 13. William, son of William and Sarah Millett. 6 years. Died very suddenly, suffering a fever. She a daughter of Jonathan Archer. Five children left, one son. Essex, corner of Pleasant street.

848. Oct. 18. Antony Silver. Fever, abroad, 28 years. Was with Capt. D. Smith in Surinam. Was a Portuguese and had been seven years in America. He married, at 26, Mary Longaway who was the widow of Pascal, a Frenchman, by whom she had one child. Essex, corner of lower Turner street.

849. Oct. 20. Male child of Benjamin and Mary Silver. Atroph. infan., 3 weeks. The mother a Bullock and long indisposed. They have two children, females. Daniels street below Derby.

850. Oct. 29. Elizabeth of William and Abigail Parker. Fever, 23 months. Not long sick. She a Watson, he from Bradford. Two children left, one son. Essex, between Union and Herbert streets.

851. Nov. 8. Sarah, widow of Joseph Browne. Paralytic, 80 years. Lived fifteen months after first stroke of palsy. She was a Cox, and married in 1753 at the age of twenty-five years. After eight years her husband was lost at sea off Long Island, N. Y. Two children, a son Capt. Joseph Browne, and a dau. Sarah, wife of Capt. James Chever. Essex opposite Hardy street.

852. Nov. 25. Susanna, wife of Col. Samuel Archer. Dropsy, 38 years. She a daughter of B. Babbidge, son of Madam the schooldame. She married at 20 years of age, and left six children, two males. He a son of Samuel Archer. Pleasant street off Washington Square.

853. Dec. 4. Maria, dau. of John and Susanna Paterson. Nervous fever, etc., 5 years, 6 months. With nervous fever I find dropsy in the head. She a Eulen. They have two children, females. This the eldest child. Grandmother, widow Goss.

854. Dec. 6. Thomas Groves, mariner from Ireland. Derangement, 28 years. He had been in America about seven years. Said he came from Baltimore, Ireland.

855. Dec. 7. Ebed, son of Ebed Stoddart. Drowned, 21 years. Coming from a vessel in the Harbor. Taken up on Thursday, Dec. 10 and buried on Friday. See D. B. He was the oldest child. Six children, two sons, left. She from Hingham. The family from Hingham.

856. Dec. 8. John Raftlin from Ireland. Debility, 36 years. He came to Newfoundland in his youth and found his way into the states, a pilgrim seven years in U. S.

857. Dec. 13. Sarah, dau. of Jonathan and Sarah Brown. Worms, 13 years. She a Twisse. They have two sons left. Allen's farm at Neck.

858. Dec. 15. Benjamin Brown. Drowned, coming ashore on the flats, 35 years. See D. B. Probably from North Britain.

DEATHS IN 1808.

859. Jan. 1. Albert, son of Benjamin and Mary H. Bray. Dropsy in the head, 7 months. This disorder was formerly unknown, or not described as at present. She was an Ellison, and has six children, four males. His mother a Becket. Hardy street, between Essex and Derby.

860. Jan. 1. John Johnson, mariner from Sweden. Bleeding, 42 years. A man of great animal strength, supposed burst a blood-vessel, complaining at times and several months before death. He married, at 39, a Valpy. He had been seven years in America and had one child, male, by his wife who was widow Creely. Below English street near Crowninshield's wharf.

861. Jan. 3. Sarah, widow of John Johnson. Complication, 37 years. Some time sick. She a Valpy, and married, at 18, her first husband James Creely from Ireland, with whom she lived thirteen years, and by whom she had four children, one son. Married Johnson at 34, by whom she has one son. Below English, as above.

862. Jan. 6. John McEwen. Fever, 43 years. Was from Scotland, lived at Kennebunk and came to Salem

seven years ago. He married, at 26, Hanna Townsend. Their four children in good families. He well educated.

863. Jan. 7. Male child of William and Mary Crispin. Fever, 14 months. She a Dawson. Have nine children, one son. South fields, opposite Harbor street.

864. Jan. 15. Hannah B. of Robert and Hannah Peele. Burned, 7 years. Child before the fire with cotton clothes. Mother sick in bed. Clothes caught, much burned in arms, breast, belly and back. Died in four days of mortification. She a Benson. They have three children left, one daughter. He a son of W. Peele. Mother a Becket.

865. Feb. 4. Elizabeth Brown. Aged, 73 years. Three brothers, William, James and John, were born near Brown's pond on old road to Boston. Elizabeth was the daughter of James.

866. Feb. 11. Alexander, son of Alexander and Elizabeth Buchanan. Burned, 14 months. See D. B. She was a Lane formerly a Getchel by marriage. She has two children, one son by Getchel. English street.

867. Feb. 15. Capt. John Macmellan. Fever, 71 years. He was from Scotland, and for seven years before he came to America was in the service of Great Britain, in the Navy. Twice married. First, at 35 years of age, a Bullock, with whom he lived eight years; second wife, widow Hill, with whom he lived twenty-seven years. By first wife had two children, one daughter and one son. He was remarkable for his shrewdness, uneducated, but a favored son of nature. Derby street, cor. of Turner.

868. Feb. 22. Daniel Cloutman. Apoplexy, 67 years. Twice married. First at 23 years of age, and lived nineteen years in marriage. Three children, daugh-

ters, by first wife. Second wife Mary Pierce, with whom he lived twenty-two years. Turner street.

869. Mar. 11. News of the death of Capt. Daniel Ropes. Fever abroad, 42 years. He was cast away on coast of England. He had been sick, suffered in the storm and died after he reached London, Jan. 12. He married, at 24, Alice Chever. Has left two children, one son. Essex, cor. of Daniels street.

870. Apr. 11. Hannah, widow of Capt. Samuel Webb. Fever, 72 years. She was a granddaughter of Deacon Ward. Her father John Ward. She was second wife of Capt. Webb and lived twenty-two years in marriage; the first wife a Prince. Her last illness of a few days. Much esteemed. He a grandson of Deacon Webb of Second Church, and died in 1780. One son at home, one daughter, Hosmer, at Norwich, Conn. Pleasant, cor. of East street.

871. Apr. 15. Hon. Jacob Crowninshield, esq. Consumption, 38 years. Was a member of Congress. Left his wife in 1807, and died at Washington, during session of Congress. See D. B. He was son of George, son of John and of John. Married, at 27, a daughter of John Gardner. Left four children, two sons. Derby street, cor. of Union.

872. Apr. 23. Benjamin, child of Benjamin and Mary Patterson. Chincough, 9 weeks. Some time afflicted with the cough. He a son of the late William Patterson. She a daughter of Major Barnes. One child, a daughter, left. Herbert street.

873. May 4. Sarah, wife of Samuel Haseltine, mariner. After delivery, 20 years. She married at 17, and was a daughter of Palfrey, sailmaker. He a son of Haseltine, sexton. Left a child, male. Essex, between Curtis and Orange streets.

874. May 5. William, son of Thomas Peach and Lydia Reeves. Throat distemper and scarlet fever, 4 years. Sick a few days. He was a grandson of Robert Smith near the bridge, *alias* ferry. She a Munnion. She left two daughters; he, two sons. Pleasant street, near Bridge.

875. May 26. Thomas Street, mariner. Complaints in the chest, 37 years. Mr. Street had a complaint in the legs which was removed and ended in complaints which resembled dropsy in chest. Confined some time. He married, at 28, Sarah Edwards whose mother was a daughter of Rev'd S. Fiske. He was from Long Island, N. Y. Four children, two sons. English street.

876. May 28. Elizabeth, wife of Dr. Moses Little. Consumption, 34 years. Long sick. Seven brothers and three sisters survive her. She a daughter of G. Williams, merchant, and was married at 24. He from Newbury. Children, two sons. Essex street, between Elm and Liberty.

877. June 3. Benjamin Bray, shipwright. Consumption, 33 years. Grandson of John Bray. A worthy man. His mother Eunice Becket. His wife an Ellison, whom he married at 19 years of age. Six children left, four sons and two daughters. Hardy street, Mr. Diman's house.

878. July 27. Capt. Jonathan Mason. Consumption, 51 years. Of a primitive family. First wife a King, with whom he lived thirteen years; second a King, dau. of Benjamin, with whom he lived fifteen years. He left two daughters by first wife, one married a Rhue. Had and left five children, two males, by a second wife. Lived in Northfields. See D. B.

879. Aug. 13. Margaret, widow of Capt. Edward Allen. Intermittent fever, 54 years. She was a Lock-

hart of North Carolina. Came to Salem thirty years ago. She was very young to her husband. Married at 23, living in marriage twenty-five years. Four children survive her, two sons. Capt. Allen's first wife was a Hodges by whom he had three children, one son. A grandchild also, Mary Swett, by deceased daughter, a Webb. Lived partly on her farm on Salem Neck. Derby street, cor. of Hardy. See D. B.

880. Aug. 22. Emma, dau. of Abraham and Emma Vikery. Worms, 6 years. Six days' illness. Father from Marblehead, mother a Williams. One child left. Essex street, near Becket.

881-2. Aug. 31. Maria Antoinetta, dau. of Abraham and Emma Vikery. Dysentery, 3½ years; Mary, dau. of William and Mary Patterson. Sisters, widows, in one house. Williams. They had between them three children, Aug. 22. No children left. Essex street, between Turner and Becket.

883. Sept. 3. Lydia, wife of Thomas Masury. Consumption, 42 years. Married at 22. He of Salem, she a Swasey. Left three children, all sons.

884. Sept. 8. William, son of Samuel and Susanna Caban. Dysentery, 18 months. Sick four days after the whooping cough. She a Rhue, dau. of Thomas Rhue. Two children left, one son. Turner street, between Derby and Essex.

885. Sept. 9. Edward, son of Samuel and Lydia Leach. Dysentery, 2 years, 7 months. Sick four days after the whooping cough. She a Becket, dau. of Retire Becket. Four children, three sons. Turner street, below Derby.

886. Sept. 9. John Ruttledge, son of Richard and Ann Crowninshield. Dysentery, 6 months. Sick four days after whooping cough. She from New York, a

Sterling. From Sligo, Ireland, a widow O'Brien. Five children, three sons. Derby street, between English and Webb.

887. Sept. 12. Samuel Hobbes, son of Samuel and Sarah Briggs. Dysentery, 11 months. Sick four days without cough. She a Hobbes. Grandmother a Phippen. Only child. Young couple. Union street.

888. Sept. 14. Edward Tuttle, son of William and Mary Foye. Dysentery, 3 years. After four days, with whooping cough. She a Collins. Married a Ledbetter, then Foye. Fourteen children between them, seven males. Essex street, below English.

889. Sept. 16. Nehemiah Holt, son of Daniel and Mary Proctor. Dysentery, 1 year, 9 months. About four days sick. She a Holt. He from Danvers. One child left, a son; husband absent. Union street.

890. Sept. 16. Mary, wife of Joseph Crookshanks. Dysentery, 64 years. Complaining some time. Confined four days. A very corpulent woman. She a Johnson from Marblehead, and lived in Lynn. Married, at 22, first in 1766 a Newell, with whom she lived 19 years, and by whom she had one child. He died in 1785, and she married, second, in 1786, J. Crookshanks, who died in 1794. Hardy street, near East Meeting House.

891. Sept. 21. Lydia, wife of Jacob Hayes. Cramp, 49 years. Thrice married. Married 1st at 19, and lived twelve years in marriage; 2nd, ten years and 3rd, four years. She from Wilmington, N. C. He from Prussia. She had two children by Webb, one son. Daughter Anna married W. Price in 1804. Derby street, near Daniels.

892. Sept. 26. Martha Silsbee, dau. of Daniel and Deborah Sage. Dysentery, 1 year. After four days. He from Scotland, she a daughter of S. Silsbee. Three

children, one daughter. Essex street, near East Meeting House.

893. Oct. 20. Mary Ann, dau. of Haven and Mary Poole. Disorder in the head, 3 years, 7 months. She was a Chapman. He named for Rev'd Haven of Reading, whence he came. Two children left. Essex street, near old Meeting House, near centre of town.

894. Oct. 21. Samuel Hobbes, son of Samuel and Sarah Briggs. Convulsions, soon after birth. He a son of Capt. Johnson Briggs. She a Hobbes. This their second child. First died last month. Union street.

895. Oct. 28. Juliana, dau. of Jacob and Ruth Endicott. Burned, 3 years. Playing near the fire which caught its clothes, and before help, much burned, and died in twenty-four hours. He from Danvers, seven generations from Gov. Endicott. One child left. Between Pleasant and Brown streets.

896. Nov. 25. Mehitable, wife of Clifford Byrne. Rheumatic affections, 36 years. She was the only daughter of Capt. William Patterson. Married, at 23 ; a woman of uncommon merit and sufferings. See D. B. Left two daughters. Herbert street.

897. Dec. 16. Mary N., dau. of John and Mary Peters. Dropsy in head, 8 years. Child long sick, some suppose fever. She an Archer, married first a Gunnerson by whom she had one child, a son; second, a Norman; then Peters, by whom she had one child. He of the ancient family of Peters. Bridge street.

DEATHS IN 1809.

898. Jan. 1. Hannah Francks, a maiden. Lockjaw, 32 years. No evident cause can be assigned for the tetanus by the best medical aid. Her father came from Cor-

sica and her mother from Jersey, Rachel, dau. of John and Mary Aubin, *née* Nicolls. A son and two daughters left. Hannah born in Andover. See D. B. Becket street.

899. Jan. 16. Charlotte, wife of Capt. James Fairfield. Convulsions, 25 years. Married at 22, and dau. of Capt. S. Goodrich of Beverly. Two children, one male. Becket street.

900. Feb. 4. William Karn (properly Caln). Palsy, 37 years. Infirm. He from Scotland, Clyde. Married at 34. She a Gotier, widow Fletcher, then married Caln. No children.

901. Feb. 23. Elizabeth, widow of Josiah Gaines. Aged, 83 years. Married at 20 years of age, and fifty years in marriage. She was a Hamatt of Boston. See D. B. Had bountiful friends, was a long time feeble and subject to transient deliriums, but of good character and mild manners. Her husband, Josiah Gaines, died in May, 1796, æt. 76. He came from Boston in the siege of 1775. A ropemaker. Winter, off Bridge street.

902. Mar. 1. Margaret, widow of John Young. Aged 90 years. She was an Abbott. Twice married; 1st, in 1744, at 25, Joseph Silsbey, and lived sixteen years with him. Married, second, John Young, in 1770, with whom she lived eight years. See D. B. Abbot's Cove named from her grandfather. She was born in the year that the meeting-house was built. Williams street at Widow Ross'.

903. Mar. 9. Nathaniel Phippen. Consumption, 44 years. He was a son of Joshua Phippen, and married, at 21, a Picket of Beverly. After marriage, he lived at Portsmouth. Cooper. Left four sons and three daughters. Derby street, between Hardy and Daniels.

904. Mar. 14. Elizabeth, wife of Benjamin Waters.

Consumption, 27 years. She was the daughter of Capt. John Becket by his second wife, an Ingersoll, and married at 23 years of age. Derby street, below Becket.

905. Mar. 21. Elizabeth Philpot, maiden. Cancer, 88 years. Lived with her sister but died at her own house. See D. B. Example of longevity of maiden. Of sober and industrious habits. Essex street, not far above Pleasant.

906. Mar. 23. Mary, widow of Pasca Foot. St. Anthony's fire, 83 years. Daughter of Joseph and Ruth Mascoll. Baptized Oct. 3, 1725. Twice married. At 19, in 1744, she married a Tapley with whom she lived four years; in 1753 she married a Foot with whom she lived nineteen years and by whom she had two daughters, who married Southward and Clearage. She had also a child by her first husband. Essex street, between Turner and Carlton.

907. Mar. 28. Abigail, of Zechariah and Abigail Curtis. Debility, 69 years. Married late in life a Jenkins.

908. Apr. 10. Maria, of Antony and Mary Silver. Worms, 16 months. He a foreigner, dead. She a Longeway and widow Pascal. One child by former husband. Her father Jeremy Longeway, Her mother a Ruewing of Neutral French. Hardy street, between Essex and Derby.

909. Apr. 13. Priscilla, dau. of Nicholas and Nancy Lane. 18 years. Derby street between Carlton and Becket.

910. April 24. Sara of Benjamin and Elizabeth Dodd. Laudanum, administered and sold for Elix. Sal., 6 months. Three cents were sent to Dr. Lang and thirty cents worth of laudanum sent and unintentionally administered. Child lived eighteen hours. She was a Smith from Marblehead. They have four children, two males. St. Peter's street.

911. Apr. 28. George son of John and Elizabeth Hill. Fever with atrophy, 12 months.. She a dau. of W. Browne. Seven children left, five males. Corner of Charter and Fish streets in Market street.

912. May 5. Mary, wife of Benjamin Silver. Mortification in the bowels, 31 years. Long infirm and never in good health. She a Bullock and married at 21. A descendant from Rev'd Ulmer, who came from Germany to Maine. Left two children, males. Turner street, between Essex and Derby.

913. May 8. Jonathan, male child of Israel and Mary Ward. Dropsy in the head, 11 months. The dropsy in head takes the place of nervous complaints, anything not well understood. She a Murray. Two children left, females. Becket street.

914. May 29. Mehitable, wife of John Dyseton. Consumption, 31 years. She was of the family of Masury, and married at 28. He from Denmark, Copenhagen, mariner, called Dystill. Two children left, one male. At the Bridge from Neptune to Water street.

915. June 19. Eunice, wife of Samuel Tucker. Consumption, 40 years. Had been a nurse in Jacob Crowninshield's family, and much esteemed by him, and remembered in his will. She was a Stevens, married at 23 years of age, and time in marriage 12 years; her mother a Mascoll, now widow Welman. She had been a widow five years. Four children, three males. Derby street, corner of Becket.

916. June 28. Female child of Joel and Hanna Potter. At birth. She was a Lufkin. Two children left, one male. Derby street corner of Becket.

917. July 5. Ruth, wife of Capt. Christopher Babbidge. Consumption, 41 years. She was a Randall of Old York, Me., and lived eleven years in Capt. Allen's

family, and married at 24. Seven children, two sons. Becket street.

918. July 25. Jacob Manning, son of Thomas Bickford. Fever, 4 years. After measles, fever. Mother a Manning, dead. Living with the father's brother John Bickford who married Mary Ramsdall. Two children left, sons. Bridge street.

919. July 26. News of the death of Benjamin, son of Benjamin Hutchinson. Fever, 19 years. Died at Havana in Cuba, from ship Adeline, Allen master. Wife Elizabeth Hitchins. Father died, July, 1805. Two sons left. Parents live in Turner below Derby street.

920. Aug. 4. Mary Lane, dau. of Nathaniel and Sara Delano. Convulsions after measles, 7 years. She a daughter of Nicholas Lane. Four children left, three sons. Derby street, corner of English.

921. Aug. 16. Sara, dau. of James and Elizabeth Archer. Convulsions, 17 years. Recovering from fever, able to rise and sit up, when she was seized with violent convulsions and expired. She a daughter of John Archer, he a son of Jonathan Archer. Three children left, two sons. Essex street, cor. of Pleasant.

922. Aug. 17. Lydia, dau. of Lemuel and Sarah Philips. Atrophy, seven months. He from Londonderry. She a Carrol of Salem. One daughter left. Bridge street, near Beverly Bridge.

923. Oct. 22. Nancy, dau. of William and Mary Crispin. Worn out, 22 years. Mother a Dawson. Mr. Crispin is a rigger, with ten children still left. Had fourteen. South fields.

924. Nov. 1. Mary, dau. of David and Sarah Newhall. Quinsy, after measles, 2½ years. She a Dunckly of Danvers. One child left, a female. Derby street, below English.

925. Nov. 9. Geffroy Moritz. Dropsy, 43rd year. Baptized Jan. 11, 1767. Dismissed from army in 1805, arrived from Dusseldorf in 1805. Residence passes of same date. Had not been long in Salem from Surinam. See D. B. Turner street, below Derby.

926. Nov. 9. Capt. James Cole of Saco. Fever, 39 years. His wife from Saco at the funeral. Arrived in Salem, sick, Nov. 5, Sunday last, from Antigua, West Indies, and had not had proper care. Commander of the brig Romeo. Six children. Derby street, near English.

927. Dec. 10. News of death of Joseph, son of Joseph and Mary Brown. Fever abroad, 19 years. She a Becket. Six children, four males. Essex street, fronting Pleasant.

928. Dec. 25. Charles, son of James and Charlotte Fairfield. Quinsy, 1 year. She a Goodrich of Beverly, died in January last. One child left, a son. Becket street.

929. Dec. 27. Samuel, son of James and Mary Clift. Quinsy, 8 months. Child sick five days. She a Masury. Clift, son of Clift, a man of humor, from Ireland. One child left, a female. English street.

DEATHS IN 1810.

930. Jan. 7. Richard Collins, from Ireland. Found dead in bed, 72 years. He came directly to Salem from Newfoundland in 1763, and married, at 32, Mary Cox, widow Cotton. Left two daughters. Daniels street.

931. Jan. 7. News of the death of Thomas Shatswell. By a fall, 28 years. Mate of a ship; hurt himself by a fall. Carried into England, and died at Yarmouth, in a high state of derangement. Married, at 23, a Rowell,

whose mother was a Becket. Two children, one male. Turner street.

932. Jan. 20. Susanna Beadle, maiden. Suddenly, 80 years. Born, by family record, Aug. 7, 1729. Of an ancient Salem family. At twenty-five she went into the family of Abraham Watson, left in 1759.

933. Feb. 14. John, son of John and Sara Becket. Atrophy, 15 months Only child. She a Brown, dau. of James Brown by a Masury. He son of Capt. John Becket. Becket street.

934. Mar. 11. News of the death of Philip Allen. Drowned, 23 years. Drowned on his passage from Europe. He was from Dresden, Me. In Salem two years. He was married at 22. His wife Mary Williams, of Salem, married W. Patterson, and lived with him four months, and he died at sea. One child, son, by Allen. Water street.

935. Mar. 15. Sara, wife of James Grey. Fever, 65 years. She was a Whitefoot of Salem, and married at 30 years of age. Her husband had a former wife, Cressy, of Beverly. They have lived many years at Pest House on the Neck. A most faithful woman. One son.

936. Mar. 26. Benjamin Millet, hardware dealer. Fever, 36 years. Married, at 22, Mary, dau. of William Peele. From the old family of Hardy by his mother's side. Five children, two sons. Corner of Herbert and Essex streets.

937. May 4. Mary, dau. of Stephen and Hanna Webb. Fever, 10 years. Not long sick, but violent and nervous fever, said the physician. She a Gale, he a son of the late Stephen Webb. Three children left, one male. Becket street, near Derby.

938. May 22. Samuel Webb, son of John. Con-

sumption, 41 years. Numerous family connections. He married, at 24, Abigail Palfrey. Followed the sea. His father and mother now living. Five children, two sons. Becket street.

939. June 25. Margaret Shelton, maiden. Consumption, 36 years. Her mother a Whitford, and still living.

940. July 22. News of the death of George Prince. At sea, 18 years. He was a passenger in the ship Margaret from Naples, which was upset in a squall in the Atlantic. Two boats escaped with their crews, 46 in all. Eighteen have arrived. His father Capt. H. Prince. Two sons and two daughters.

941. July 22. News of the death of John Browne, upon the wreck of the ship Margaret, 27 years. We had notice of him by the second boat. He married, at 25, an Ashby. One son.

942. Aug. 19. William Millet. Delirious, 47 years. Of an ancient family of Tozer and Millet. He was a seaman, then coaster. Was seized with delirium, which ran into downright madness at last. Above six months in confinement. Married, at 27, Sara, dau. of Jonathan Archer. One son and four daughters left.

943. Aug. 22. Sara, dau. of Timothy and Sara Welman. Consumption, 27 years. She was a worthy young woman, much lamented. His wife a Wyatt. Three sons and three daughters left.

944. Sept. 25. James Grey, mariner. Palsy, 66 years. Married at 24; first wife a Cressy, with whom he lived thirty-five years. She died in March last. Three children by first wife. The child by last wife dead.

945. Oct. 2. William, son of William and Helen Rhue. Atrophy, 14 months. Only child. The mother a daughter of the celebrated James Tytler, who emi-

grated from Scotland. Married three years. Webb street.

946. Oct. 4. William Howe, servant of Nicholas Lane. Suddenly, 61 years. He came from west of England near Dartmouth to Newfoundland. Has been with Mr. Lane twenty-nine years. A faithful servant. Had several violent spasms in one of which he probably died. Derby street, near Becket.

947. Oct. 8. Female child of Benjamin and Catharine Swasey. Atrophy, 9 months. She a Catholic, from Waterford in Ireland. Child baptized by Dr. Matisnon. No other child. Becket street.

948. Oct. 26. Jesse Perkins, laborer. Consumption, 34 years. Took cold in a well fourteen months before death and never recovered. Father and mother dead. Came with his father's family into Salem from Topsfield, and lived on Neck farm then belonging to Mr. Derby, and afterward at entrance of the Neck. Bridge street, near Beverly Bridge.

949. Nov. 18. Mary, widow of Capt. Andrew Preston. Aged 78 years. Long infirm. She was a Lambert, married in 1753, at the age of 20, Capt. Andrew Preston who died in 1799. One son and three daughters left. One daughter unmarried, one daughter widow Rantoul, and one Mrs. Lefavre. Essex street, opposite Pleasant.

950. Nov. 26. David, son of John and Mary Browne. Dropsy in head, 13 months. Father died on wreck Margaret. Mother an Ashby. One child, a daughter left. Water street.

951. Dec. 2. Capt. Timothy Welman, 54 years. He married, at 21, Sarah Wyatt. Has three sons and three daughters left. Derby street, near Hardy.

952. Dec. 19. William Brown ("Billy," so called).

Dropsy, 62 years. Mother a Tozzer, father a foreigner. Not of the ancient family of Browne.

953. Dec. 29. Mary, wife of Capt. Benjamin Ward. Fever, 61 years. She was a most worthy woman and most intimate in our family. Her only brother Thomas in New York. She a daughter of Paul Farmer of Boston, keeper of the town almshouse; married, at 26, Capt. W. Carlton in 1776, with whom she lived nineteen years; and Capt. Ward in 1801, with whom she lived nine years. No children. Essex street, opposite Daniels.

DEATHS IN 1811.

954. Jan. 2. Richard Manning, Esq. Aged, 80 years. A man of great wealth, never married. Left an infirm brother Jacob, and two sisters who lived with him. Essex street, between Curtis and Herbert.

955. Jan. 9. Sara, wife of Matthew Vincent. Dropsy, 40 years. Married at 20 years of age. She a daughter of Jonathan and Mary Andrew. Her mother a Gardner. His father Joseph from Kittery. Five children left, three males. Essex street, between Orange and Daniels.

956. Jan. 19. Abigail Rogers, daughter of Samuel and Priscilla Lambert. Scrofula, 6 months. Mother a dau. of Joseph Lambert. Three children left, one son. Essex street, below Pleasant, near Daniels.

957. Jan. 24. Samuel Masury. Drowned, 59 years. He was acting as pilot to a ship outward bound. See D. B. for the event. He was in command of the Revenue Boat. Married, at 27, Elizabeth Webb, daughter of Stephen. Left six children. English street.

958. Jan. 31. Mary, widow of Timothy Welman. Cholera morbus, 74 years. She a Henderson, married at

18, and lived thirteen years in marriage. Husband died on the Banks, lost. Four daughters left, Phippen, Dean, Driver and Swasey. Son died in December last. Essex, near English street.

959. Jan. 31. Sara, widow of Jonathan Millet. Suddenly, 76 years. Died immediately upon a return from a visit without any sign of pain or alarm. She was of the family Mansfield. Married, at 23, in 1758, and lived in married life thirty-seven years. Husband died in 1795, born in 1735. Left three daughters. Essex street, cor. of Herbert.

960. Mar. 16. Pickering Collins. Asthma, 69 years. Married, at 30 years of age, a Morgan and lived on the farm which had been her father's in South Fields. His mother, daughter of Capt. Pickering and sister to Mrs. Watson. One son, single. Near Gardner's Mills, Salem.

961. Apr. 5. Dorcas, widow of Matthew Calley. Fever, 57 years. She was a Kane. Married first, at 15, an Aden, with whom she lived seven years; then Calley with whom she lived three years. Children by both, but none living. Grandchildren survive. Summer street.

962. Apr. 23. Mary, wife of William Foye and widow of David Ledbetter. Consumption, 48 years. Married first, at 18, a Ledbetter, with whom she lived six years; then W. Foye, with whom she lived thirteen years. She was a Collins. Five children left, two sons and three daughters. English street.

963. May 6. Elizabeth, widow of Capt. Thomas Williams, 48 years. She a Babbidge. Married first, at 25, a Cotton, with whom she lived three years; lived eleven years in second marriage. Two children of Capt. Williams with her. No children of her own survived. She useful, kept a school. Hardy street.

964. May 14. Sara, widow of William Swaney. Suddenly, 48 years. Married first, at 23, in 1786, Jacob Abraham of Surinam from Boston, with whom she lived three years, and afterwards, in 1791, W. Swaney, of Ireland, with whom she lived three years. Her mother died in January last. Both husbands died abroad. A son by each left. Essex street, opposite English.

965. May 17. John Webb. Aged, 79 years. Son of deacon Jonathan Webb. Married at 20 years of age and lived together above fifty-nine years. His wife a Phelps. Left three sons and three daughters. Daniel street, below Derby street.

966. June 8. Capt. John Berry. Fever, 47 years. Fever high from the beginning, one week. He had been commander of a vessel, and was in the Custom house boat with Masury. Son of Oliver and Mary Berry. Married, at 24, a Ward whose parents were drowned in King's Boat, 1773. Left seven children, six sons. English street, near Derby.

967. June 15. Mary, widow of Richard Collins. Aged, 73 years. Daughter of Edward and Mary Cox. Married first, at 26, a Cotton, with whom she lived three years; then Collins, from Ireland, with whom she lived forty years. Two daughters by last marriage. Daniels street.

968. June 28. Haven Poole, printer. Convulsions, 29 years. He from Reading. Married, at 23, a Chapman. See Day Book. Named after Rev'd Haven of Reading. Two children, daughters. Pleasant street, between Brown and Bridge streets.

969. July 5. Clarissa, dau. of Samuel and Mary Goodrich. Fever, 9 years. Child born at Schodiac, Me., living in Salem not one year. She a Dutch from Ipswich. He from Connecticut, abroad. Three daughters left. Neptune, between Walnut and Elm streets.

970. July 15. Male child of Francis R. and Emma Branigan. 3 days. She a Williams and lately widow Victory. He a foreigner. Becket street.

971. July 28. News of the death of David Beadle, son of David and Lydia. Epilepsy, 36 years. Died at West Indies. A worthy man. His mother a Wiley. His wife, whom he married at 30, was a daughter of Samuel Silsbee. Left two sons. Webb street.

972. Aug. 1. Stephen Larabee, mariner. Liver complaint, 24 years. Married at 21. His father moved from Lynn to Danvers, where he was born. Married Judith Rhuee. Three children, two males. Becket street.

973. Sept. 1. Margaret, dau. of Benjamin and Margaret Nourse. Complication of ills, 27 years. Brought from Boston. Her father of an old family. The mother a Welcome, both of Salem.

974. Sept. 26. Cynthia, wife of Israel Andrew. Consumption, 19 years. Married at 18. She a daughter of Abijah Hitchins. Mother a Gardner. One child. English street.

975. Oct. 13. Moses Little. Consumption, 45 years. Educated at Cambridge (A. M., Camb., A. B., 1787). A physician. Born in Newbury, came to Salem in 1791. Married, at 34, a Williams who died in 1808. Essex street, between Newbury and Liberty.

976. Nov. 15. A female child in care of Michael and Mary Hardigan. Atrophy, 4 years. Michael Hardigan from Ireland. His wife's father from Ireland, a Ryan. The child said to belong to another named Smith in Boston. Two years in their care. Orange street.

977. Nov. 16. Capt. Joseph Franks. Consumption, 29 years. His father from Corsica, but been in Salem above 30 years. His mother from Isle of Jersey. His wife a

Sarah Evoy, granddaughter of Capt. Reuben Richards. The son was my charge from his infancy. One child, a male. Married life of one year. Bridge street. See D. B., 50, p. 69.

978. Dec. 6. Susanna, widow of Capt. Samuel Ingersoll. Consumption, 65 years. Married at 25. She had been long infirm, but not long confined. Left a good estate, and possessed all the pride of family. Her husband died July, 1804. She was descended from English, etc. Left an only daughter Susanna, æt. 27. Turner's House, Turner street. See D. B.

DEATHS IN 1812.

979. Jan. 28. Lydia, widow of Capt. Thomas Dean. Fever, 49 years. Her son had been sick with a fever. She was seized violently. Sick ten days. She was a daughter of Capt. Waters at the Massey House at the ferry, married at 21 years of age, and lived six years in married life. She has left two children; one son, one daughter. See D. B. Derby street, between Hardy and Turner.

980. Feb. 21. Lucia, dau. of Benj. W. and Mary Crowninshield. Convulsions, 6 weeks. Child seized five days before its death most violently. Mother a Boardman. They have left three sons and two daughters. Curtis and Orange streets, facing Derby street.

981. Feb. 24. Elizabeth, widow of John Masury. See D. B. Aged, 94 years. She a Bush. Thrice married; first, at 25, W. Phippen in 1744, with whom she lived five years; second, S. Boynall in 1749, with whom she lived seven years; third, J. Masury, in 1776, and he died in 1797. She lived, until a few years before her

death, near old Neck Gate, afterwards with her son-in-law Punchard and in his care, and died at Punchard House on Essex street, below Beckford.

932. Mar. 17. Mary, widow of Benj. Babbidge. Consumption, 41 years. Lost their property with Col. S. Archer in the speculation of that debtor. Many interested. Distress of mind ended in consumption. She a daughter of Joshua Phippen, married at 19 years, and lived twenty years in marriage. He lost at sea last year. One son survives, now at sea. Andrew street.

983. June 11. Capt. Benjamin Ward. Jaundice, 73 years. Twice married. First, at 31, Elizabeth Babbidge, who died in 1797; second, Mary, widow of W. Carlton, with whom he lived nine years, who died in 1810. Deacon for thirty years, and was the grandson of deacon Miles Ward, by Ebenezer, who died at 92. See MSS. 3014 and 1125. Essex, near Daniels street.

984. Aug. 9. Alice, widow of James Cotton. Convulsions, 49 years. She was a Welcome of Gloucester. She married first, at sixteen, a Lord, who died three years after; then a Lister with whom she lived two years; and third, a Cotton with whom she lived five years, and who perished at the Texel in 1791. None of her children known to have survived her, though their death not all certain. Very infirm. A relative of the Salem family of Welcomes.

985. Aug. 26. Rebecca, widow of Capt. William Fairfield. Rupture, 59 years. She a daughter of John Becket, married at 18, and lived eighteen years in marriage. Three sisters survive. Husband killed by slaves in 1789. Six children left, three sons; daughters Phippen and widow Reed, two sons married and two single. Allen street, between English and Webb.

986. Sept. 3. William Browne, deacon. Lethargy,

79 years. He of Salem. Thrice married. First wife, Mercy White, whom he married at 22, and lived with her thirty years, by whom his children; second, Phœbe Ganson, with whom he lived nineteen years, (she married first a Porter, then Carlton, then Browne); third, Mary Collins, with whom he lived five years, she the widow Orne. Left nine children, seven females. All have been married but one, Deacon for thirty years. Curtis street.

987. Sept. 6. Martha, dau. of William and Eunice Burrill. Consumption and scrofula, 14 years. Sick from February last. Scrofulous humor in eyes, blind for some time. He son of Mansfield Burrill from Lynn, she a Coffin married in 1791. Four children left, two sons and two daughters. Derby street, near Neck Gate.

988. Sept. 12. Female child of Susanna Davison, 14 days. Union street, Williams' *alias* Brown's house.

989. Oct. 3. Abigail, widow of Samuel Webb. Consumption, 39 years. She was a Palfrey, married at 20, and lived seventeen years with her husband who died May 22, 1810. Her father a sailmaker, living in Derby street, opposite Becket. Five children left, two sons. Near Neck Gate, Derby street.

990. Oct. 7. Richard Tannenhall, a seaman and stranger. Suddenly, 43 years. Died instantly in B. Webb's apothecary shop on Essex street. His discharge from U. S. service, 1812, said he was born in Amsterdam, came to enter into a Privateer. He told he had been married in S. C., but he had no wife nor children to provide for. His certificate from Am. Consul, London, 1808.

991. Oct. 10. Lucia Nichols, son of Nehemiah and Sara Curtis. Convulsions, 10 months. Child scalded in the arm. To relieve pain an indiscreet use of opium, whence convulsions ensued, and in four days death fol-

lowed. Both strangers in Salem, lately from Boston. One child, a female, left. Head of Union wharf.

992. Oct. 20. Eunice, wife of Jesse Richardson. Internal obstructions, 34 years. Sick nearly two years. She consulted many physicians who could not detect the cause or relieve her, journeyed, etc., but in vain. She was the eldest daughter of Joshua Dodge, esq., and married at 22. He a son of Nathaniel Richardson. She bears the name of both mothers. Seven children left, four males. Brown street, cor. of Washington Square.

993. Oct. 31. William, son of William and Eunice Burrill. Suddenly in convulsions, 17 years. Was thought to have taken cold on Wednesday. Was, on 30th, gunning in North fields; returning at sundown, complained of his head and died at midnight. His sister was buried on the 6th of September last. (See the family at that date.) He had lived in family of Rogers. One son and two daughters left. Derby street, near Neck Gate.

994. Nov. 15. Daniel Shehane, mariner. From the bursting of a cannon, 44 years. It happened Nov. 4. He broke his leg and fever ensued. Seven persons at same time in Salem Harbor. Among others, Capt. P. Townsend and J. Knapp. Married, at 22, Bethiah Wedger of Marblehead. His father from England, his mother a Masury. Left six children, five daughters. Below Essex and Becket streets.

995. Dec. 10. Nathaniel Weston. Fever, 53 years. Shoemaker. A man of good habits, but of a speculating turn of mind. Lived in Salem nineteen years. Married, at 23, a Richardson. Both of Reading. Seven children left, two sons. Derby street near Webb, water side.

996. Dec. 11. Samuel Swasey. Old age, 82 years. Shoemaker and mariner, captain. His mother died July

22, 1807, aged 100. He only survived her. Twice married. First, at 26, Elizabeth Skinner in 1756, with whom he lived three years; second, Mary Greves in 1762, with whom he lived twenty-two years. Six children left, one son and five daughters, viz.: John, Rebecca Becket, Abigail Black, Hanna Brown, Margaret Millet, Mary More, all by his last wife. Daniels street. (See D. B., L., pp. 146–7.)

997. Dec. 24. Sarah, dau. of Benjamin and Hanna Hodges. Consumption, 14 years. Taken with bleeding, lingered a month. Mother a King. Three sisters survive. This the sixth child dying of consumption. Father worthy. Youngest child. Essex street, cor. of Orange.

998. Dec. 27. Mercy, wife of Capt. Joseph Webb. Typhus fever, 41 years. Sick a short time. She was a Devereux of Marblehead, married at 23. Educated by widow Gale, a Crowninshield. Husband youngest son of Stephen Webb. He lately commanded in militia. Shipbuilder, etc. Became a merchant, etc., a year on return to his business. Left six children, three sons. Derby street, between Webb and English.

DEATHS IN 1813.

999. Jan. 20. John, son of John O. and Mehitable Dileton. Tumor in throat, 6 years. The mother, Mehitable Masury, died in 1809. In three years married May Laralle, dau. of John Knap. One child by first wife, one by second. Turner street, between Essex and Derby.

1000. Feb. 8. Philip English. Old age, 77 years. Was sexton for forty-eight years, and was able to do duty till last season. For his character see Sermons and

MSS. He was honest, faithful and obstinate. His wife Eunice Ellingwood, of Beverly, whom he married at 23, died in 1785. He left one son and two daughters. One daughter widow Waters, the other Vanderfort. Son married a Patten. All have children. Philip was the son of John, and brother of John and Joseph. Essex street, Old Gate.

1001. Feb. 21. News of the death of Stephen Webb, in the action of the Constitution with the Java, Dec. 29, 41 years. Wound from handling a cartridge, it took fire. Son of Stephen, and married, in 1796 at 23, Hannah Gale. Eccentric. An excellent seaman. Left three children, two youngest in the ship.

1002. Mar. 1. John Thresher. Fever, 22 years. Born in Beverly, and his father and family removed from Beverly to Salem. Of the 4th Reg., U. S. A. Was in Hull's army; taken at Detroit upon parole and died at home in Daniels street.

1003. Mar. 4. Mary, widow of Capt. John Batten. Aged, 80 years. She had been long infirm, but not confined by sickness but for a short time. Much esteemed. Married at 25, living twenty-three years in married life. Husband died in 1781. His sister Sayward now living in the house. Left a daughter, widow Bateman, schoolmistress, and children of a deceased son. Husband's brother living at Lyndeborough, N. H. Turner street, between Derby and Essex.

1004. Mar. 9. Abigail, dau. of Nathaniel and Abigail Chever. Dropsy in head, 13 months. She a Hutchinson. Four children left. Turner street, below Derby.

1005. Apr. 8. Mary Tozzer, a maiden. Aged, 77 years. She has a sister Patterson living, above ninety years of age, and a sister-in-law above eighty years of age.

1006. Apr. 19. Richard Manning. Apoplexy, 58 years. Was on his journey to Maine. Died at Newbury. A blacksmith, stage keeper and landholder. He came to Salem with his wife from Ipswich in 1776. See D. B., L. 165. She was Miriam Lord. Married at 21. Nine children left, five sons. Union and Herbert streets.

1007. Apr. 20. Dorothy, dau. of Richard Palfrey. Fever, 22 years. Died in Salem. Sister to Abigail Webb who died October last. Four brothers and two sisters by same mother left. One son settled in Baltimore. Derby street.

1008. Apr. 22. News of the death of David, son of James and Sara Chever. From wounds, 20 years. On board the John, Capt. Fairfield, from Salem, while in the cabin writing, wounded by a splinter from a shot in chase from an English 74, Feb. 7. Died Feb. 12 at Barbadoes. They have three sons and three daughters left. She a Browne.

1009. May 29. Debora, wife of Mark (Maservey, so called) Servi. Fever, 37 years. She a Lambert. Married 1st, at twenty years of age, time in marriage five years; 2nd, time in marriage, two years; 3rd marriage, three years; 4th, two years. He a Genoese, in Crowninshield's employ. One daughter left by Holmes. Becket street.

1010. May 29. Joseph, child of Joseph and Sarah Guillen. Atroph. inf., 4 days. She a Crispin, widow Johnson when last married, Nov. 1, 1812. A Creole, and he from West Indies. First and only child. Old Neck street.

1011. June 4. Male child of John and Susan Lapature. Atroph. inf., 1 year, 18 days. She an Edey. Married eighteen months. Husband a Frenchman.

1012. June 13. Mary, dau. of Samuel and Eunice Moses. Lung fever, 18 months. She a Chever by P. English's daughter. He a son of Joseph Moses. One child, a daughter, left. County street.

1013. Aug. 6. Charles, son of Jesse and Eunice Richardson. By hot water thrown from a window, 2 years. Died in twenty-four hours. Mother lately deceased. Six children left, three males. Brown street, near Washington Square.

1014. Aug. 14. Ebenezer, son of Ebenezer and Elizabeth Phippen. Cholera morbus, 36 years. He was the grandson of deacon David Phippen and son of Ebenezer. Not married. A blockmaker with Mr. Jonathan Smith, and journeyman. Liberty street, between Charter and Water.

1015. Aug. 26. Margaret, sister of Richard Manning, esq. Aged, 79 years. She, with two brothers, father and sister, lived together half a century. The elder brother had a good estate. She, with one brother and one sister, lived upon an estate left by Richard Manning, esq. Had no physician, gradual decay. See D. B. Essex street, between Orange and Herbert.

1016. Aug. 28. Martha Wright. Fever, 17 years. Sick one fortnight at Mr. Upton's and buried from his son's, corner of Daniel and Essex streets. Living in the family of Mr. Upton on the Forest river farm, Salem side. Father and mother at Paxton. Two brothers and three sisters left. From Southfields.

1017. Sept. 11. Thomas, son of John M. and Rebecca Peck. Dropsy in head, 6 months. He from Danbury in Connecticut, mother living. She a Silsbee having parents and grandmother living in Salem. One child, son, left. Webb street.

1018. Sept. 27. William Jackson, son of W. and Mary Richardson. Dropsy in head, 2 months. She a Watts. One child left. Daniels street, below Derby, near the Point.

1019. Oct. 14. Philip Cotel. Fever and rupture, 32 years. He from Marblehead. Father a Frenchman. She a Mascoll and widow of Jesse Kenny. She had two children, son and daughter, by Kenny; one son by Cotel. Essex street, between Becket and English.

1020. Oct. 31. John Watson. Palsy and apoplexy, 67 years. Schoolmaster thirty-four years, public and private. His parents left him in easy circumstances, and he left off his school in 1801. He was from the Watsons of Cambridge. His father came young to Salem. By his mother from Pickering and Browne. Left four children, two sons, one in Portland unmarried. Died in Northfields.

1021. Nov. 4. Male child of Benjamin and Betsy Pierce. Atrophy inf., 9 weeks. She a Peach. He a ropemaker, now at New York. Served with Vincent. Three children left, one son and two daughters. Union street.

1022. Nov. 6. Capt. Nathaniel Chever. Consumption, 36 years. Son of Daniel Chever, well known in Salem. His mother had many sons, two survive. His wife a Hutchinson. Four children left, three males. Turner street, below Derby.

1023. Nov. 16. Hanna, wife of Capt. William Webb. Paralytic affections, 48 years. She was an Allen from Marblehead, and was brought up in Col. Pickman's family. A worthy woman. See D. B. Left four children, one son and three daughters. Hardy street, near Meeting-house.

1024. Nov. 26. Mary, wife of G. Crowninshield. Paralytic affections, 76 years. She was a dau. of Richard

Derby, esq., the last of his children. Married at 19 years of age; time in marriage fifty-seven years. Left four sons and two daughters; one married N. Silsbee. Derby street, cor. of Orange street; house built by Ropes.

1025. Dec. 5. Male child of Capt. James and Deborah Fairfield. Quinsy, about 3 years. He a son of John. She a second wife, sister of the first, a Goodrich, of Beverly. Her only child; a son by former wife. Becket street.

1026. Dec. 23. Ephraim Croswell. Fever, 18 years. A stranger, at Mrs. Tripp's. Came up from Saco to go in a Privateer, having been out in the "Stark". Said he belonged to Boston, but his parents dead; been in Salem eight weeks. Cor. Becket and Essex streets.

DEATHS IN 1814.

1027. Jan. 18. Rebecca, widow of William Patterson. Old age, 90 years. She a Tozzer. Her son William died Sept. 6, 1793, æt. 47. A most worthy man. She died by insensible decay, lay and slept like a child. Her mother died in Orange street, where my family lived, aged 85, July 1785, in the same manner. She has left three daughters. Brown street, northwestern corner Washington Square.

1028. Jan. 21. Hanna, wife of James Parker. Complication, 32 years. She was a Smith, married at 19 years of age, and lived thirteen years in marriage. Her mother a Stone. Was married from the family of Joseph Peabody, merchant. Husband's mother a Harthorne. Two daughters, one at Beverly and one at Salem.

1029. Feb. 10. News of the death of Capt. John Allen, at Halifax, Jan. 16, aged 35 years. He was a twin with his brother Alexander, who died before him, and son of the late Capt. Edw. Allen by second wife Lockart. He married 1st, at 22 years, a Nicholson from Plymouth, living with her five years; 2nd a Gardner who survives him. Two children, one by each marriage, left.

1030. Feb. 11. Jesse Richardson, merchant, 37 years. See D. B. He married, at 23, Eunice Dodge, daughter of Joshua Dodge, esq. Six children left, three males. East street, at the homestead.

1031. Feb. 12. Benjamin, son of Benjamin and Lydia Howard. Atroph. inf., 7 weeks. She a nurse in the family of Herbert Harthorne, merchant, of Salem. Husband in sea service. Two children left, one male. Turner street, below Derby.

1032. Feb. 26. Eliza, dau. of Richard Palfrey. Consumption, 22 years. This the third within a few years; Abigail in 1811, Dorothy in Apr., 1812. Four sons and a daughter left by mother of this daughter, who was a Wedger. Four children by another wife, who was a Morgan. One brother in Baltimore. Derby street, near Becket.

1033. Feb. 27. Female child of Thomas and Sara Dean, 3 days. This their first child. She a Burdett. Mother descended from Massey, Williams, and Brown. She a sister and brother. He the grandchild of Capt. Thomas Dean, and has a sister. Mrs. Williams lived long in Union street. Grandmother, sister of the mother of Mr. Dean, married Gamaliel Hodges; another sister Capt. Swett. East street.

1034. Mar. 1. Mary, widow of Capt. John Whitford. Aged, 80 years. She was a Foot, married at 23, and lived twenty years in married life. Husband died in Halifax prison in 1779. One daughter left, who married W. Oliver. One daughter married a Hill, then a Goldsmith. Left nine great grandchildren and five grandchildren. A woman of good behavior and steady mind. Derby street, corner of Webb.

1035. Mar. 19. Capt. Samuel Chever. Paralytic, 76 years. Married at 32 years, and lived forty-four years in married life. Left the sea service twenty-seven years ago. She from Black point, Scarborough, Me., and fourteen years younger than he. One daughter left, widow Beckford, who has one child. Grandchildren by a son deceased. Brown street, cor. of Winter.

1036. Mar. 20. Elizabeth, widow of David Mansfield. Mortification from broken limb, 75 years. She was a Wallace from Wilmington, N. C., married at 27, and lived thirty-one years in married life. Husband lost at sea in 1798. Had no children. See D. B. 50, p. 222.

1037. Mar. 24. Mary, wife of Israel Ward. Consumption, 34 years. Only child of Peter and Mary Murray, married at 23, and lived eleven years in married life. Always of feeble constitution, long confined. A good wife. She left three children, all males. Her mother a Webb. She heir to Aunt Cowen, known proverbially among us as Aunt Cowen's daughter. Born where she lived, Becket street.

1038. Mar. 30. Margaret, widow of William Sheldon. Palsy, 74 years. Twice married. First, at 19 years, Paul Mansfield with whom she lived seven years; second, William Sheldon, with whom she lived three years. She was a Whitford. Her children, by both husbands, died before her.

1039. April 30. Richard Palfray, sailmaker. Consumption, 69 years. Married at 21, and lived thirty-one years in married life. He was from Gloucester, descended from Capt. Robinson who built the schooner. Lived with a relative at Boston; left and came to Marblehead, and after marriage to Salem. Four sons and one daughter. Derby street, opp. Becket.

1040. May 15. Edward, son of John and Eunice Harwood. Atrophy, 17 months. The child a twin, never in good health. They have two children left, one son. Both parents born in Salem. Union street.

1041. May 20. Maria, dau. of Richard and Mariam Manning. Cynanche (see D. B.), 27 years. Father died in April, 1813, leaving nine children, five sons. Came from Ipswich in 1776. (See at that date.) The four daughters have lived with the mother. This daughter lost her voice for a year; at last the disorder, attended with general debility, ended in cynanche, for which she had the most able physicians at Boston and Salem, four of whom were with her when she died. Herbert street.

1042. May 22. Joseph, son of Joseph and Sara Guillon. Atrophy, 3 weeks. He a Frenchman and lived long with Mr. Greenleaf. Has been in the America. She a Johnson. They have one child, a daughter, left. Married nearly two years. English street.

1043. June. News of the death of Daniel, son of Daniel and Elsey Ropes. In prison. 19 years. Was taken in the ship Montgomery, carried to Halifax, thence sent to England, and died at Chatham, a prisoner, Feb. 9, 1814. His mother a Chever. Father dead. She has one child left, a daughter, who married an Upton. Mother lives in Daniels street.

1044. June. News of the death of Christopher, son of Christopher and Ruth Babbidge. In prison. 21 years. He was prizemaster of a prize to the Polly, taken and carried to Halifax, thence sent to England. Died at Chatham a prisoner, Jan. 19, 1814. He addressed a Miss Gerard. Mother a Randall. One son and five daughters left. Father's family live in Becket street.

1045. July 5. Rebecca, wife of Neal Mackey. Fever and mortification, 25 years. She was married at 18 and lived seven years in married life. From Boston and lived at Brookline, Mass. Her family name Bates. He from Boston, afterwards at Townsend, Me. He a recruiting officer at head of Crowninshield's wharf. Lived in Salem but a few years. Four children left, one daughter. Derby street, near Becket, between Becket and English.

1046. July 27. Samuel Moses, shoemaker. Consumption, 29 years. Grandson of Capt. Moses of the King's Customs. Married, at 21, a granddaughter of Philip English, sexton, and lived in married life eight years. His father Joseph died in Boston. Left a wife and two children, one son and one daughter the youngest. County street.

1047. Aug. 2. News of the death of Capt. John Bickford. Abroad at Montevideo and Buenos Ayres, 49 years. He has been detained about three years by the war, with a great property for Lt. Gov. Gray in Spanish America. Said to have died of consumption, after a fall from a horse. At 26 years of age, he married Mary Ramsdell, niece of Capt. Joseph White, and educated in his family, living twenty-three years in married life. He from Durham, N. H. Four children left, two sons. Bridge street.

1048. Aug. 17. Elizabeth, dau. of William and Hanna Webb. Fever, 19 years. A promising and really good girl. Mother a worthy woman, died November last. Children yet left one son and two daughters. Daniels street.

1049. Sept. 12. Judith, widow of John Webb, who

died May 17, 1811. Aged, 84 years. She was a Phelps, married at 21, and lived sixty years in married life. Her father lived to a great age, as did many of the family. The elder sister, Emma Southward, and the youngest sister, Eunice Perkins survive. Three sons and three daughters survive her, and many grandchildren and great-grandchildren. At her son Benjamin's on Essex, between Herbert and Union streets.

1050. Sept. 14. Isaac, of Thomas and Charlotte Magoun. Fever (affection of the head?), 7 years. He from Pembroke; she a daughter of Nicholas Lane, now of Salem, but from Gloucester. Three children, two males. Derby street, east corner of English.

1051. Sept. 23. Hiram, male child of Benjamin Hans and Mary Hancock. 5 years. Of a feeble constitution. He from Chester, Pennsylvania, nine years in Salem. She born in Danvers, a Richardson. One male child left. Carlton street.

1052. Oct. 12. Susan Farnum, twin child of Daniel and Susan Berry. Fever, 10 months. He East town schoolmaster. She a Farnum from Andover. Three children left, males. Pleasant street, opp. Washington Square.

1053. Oct. 17. Mary, widow of W. Brown. Consumption, 34 years. She was a Parnel, granddaughter of Mercy Welman, who was a Ward, and married at 19. Her mother afterwards married a Daniel. Lived in Boston and came back to Salem. One child left. Derby street, west corner of Becket.

1054. Oct. 17. Elizabeth, dau. of John Symonds, a man of a century. 86 years. Unmarried. Her father died in 1791, aged 100 years; her brother John, in 1796, aged 74 years; her sister, deceased wife of Capt. Barr. Left her estate to her benefactors and the poor. Lived near Beverly bridge, Bridge street, in a house built by her father.

1055. Oct. 21. Jonathan, son of Israel and Mary Ward. Dropsy in head (so said), 9 months. He a son of John Ward. The mother, a Murray, died in March last. Two children left, sons. Becket street.

1056. Oct. 28. Mary, dau. of William and Sara Millet. Consumption, 18 years. Long failing, not able to lie down in bed for months. Her father died in 1810. Mother an Archer. Three sisters and two brothers left. Two married to Nichols and Lawrence. Lawrence lives at Hollis. One child, male, born after death of father. Essex street, west cor. of Pleasant.

1057. Nov. 16. Hanna, widow of Capt. Benjamin Hodges. Asthma and consumption, 59 years. She was the dau. of William and Mary King, and lived in the family of Dr. Bulfinch, wife an Apmerp. Unquestionably one of the best of women. Well educated. Married at 22 years of age ; time in marriage, 28 years. She was of small person, pleasant aspect, even virtues and uniform excellence. Left three daughters, one a Silsbee. Essex street, east cor. of Orange.

1058. Dec. 17. John Collins, son of James and grandson of James. Consumption, 59 years. He married, at 29, widow Hammond, who was a Lander, and lived thirty years in marriage. Was infirm for a long time. Was one of the town watch for years. Long a prisoner which delayed marriage. His grandfather married a Becket, and his father married Sara Thomas. English street, Ingersoll's house.

1059. Dec. 18. Mary, dau. of Col. Samuel Carlton, deceased. Consumption and asthma, 47 years. She lived seventeen years with her sister Barr. Kept a public and private school. Died at her mother's, who is about

83 years old. Left two brothers and four sisters; two sisters married and one brother. Union street, or the Carlton House on old estate.

DEATHS IN 1815.

1060. Jan. 6. Margaret, widow of Daniel Curtis. Old age, 82 years. She was a Thomas of Marblehead; married at 21 years, and lived twenty-four years in married life. Was a sister of James Cotton's wife from Jersey, and lived many years a widow in English street. Came to Salem in early life; her mother a Dixey. Left no children.

1061. Jan 20. Thomas Rhue. Aged, 75 years. He married, at 24, Susanna Becket, who died in 1805; time in marriage, forty-one years. He was son of nurse Rhue, so called. Left six children, three sons and three daughters. One son and three daughters married; Kehew, Colan and Larrabee.

1062. Jan. 21. Funeral of Jeffry Allen, a prisoner from Liverpool, Eng. Consumption, 27 years. Late mate of the brig Mary of Poole. Has a wife in Liverpool, no children. Sick in the hospital for some time. Was interred with every ceremony of respect from Capt. Thomas Wells' house in County street. Capt. Wells is in the service of the Guard Ship.

1063. Feb. 1. Lydia, widow of John Teague. Consumption, 42 years. She married first, at 21, a Galloway, with whom she lived two years; time in second marriage, eight years. She was a granddaughter of Mr. Horton, who lived at Skerry's Point and after whom it was called during his life at that place.

1064. Feb. 24. Capt. Nathaniel Phippen. Consumption, etc., 57 years. Son of Deacon D. Phippen, married Apr. 20, 1779, at 21, a Hooper, with whom he lived thirty-six years. Left two children, a son, and daughter who married Capt. Jos. J. Knapp. His grandchildren by Knapp. Five sisters survive: Gill, Smith, Symonds, King, and a maiden sister. No brother left. Of an athletic constitution. Supposed injured by lodging at the Turf ground. Gardner (or March) street from Bridge street leading to Skerry's Point.

1065. Feb. 25. Hanna, dau. of Robert and Anstis Stone. Consumption, 26 years. An excellent woman, of a very delicate constitution from infancy. They have two children left; a son married and widowed daughter Sally, wife of And. Dunlap. Hardy street, near the meeting-house.

1066. Feb. 28. Jacob Manning. Long infirmities, 78 years. Never possessed health. Unmarried. Brother of Richard Manning, esq. He lived with his brother and three unmarried sisters, who are all now dead but one. Essex street, between Curtis and Herbert.

1067. Mar. 27. Jonathan, son of Thomas and Hanna Rowell, 22 years. She a Becket. Seven children survive, five sons. Turner street, between Essex and Derby.

1068. Apr. 4. Capt. Clifford Byrne. Apoplexy, 68 years. At 22, he married Margaret Whitford from Mary Elkins', and lived in married life forty-six years. Grandson of Capt. Clifford Crowninshield of Salem. Left two sons, Clifford and John, who have children. Clifford married a daughter of Capt. W. Patterson. Herbert street.

1069. Apr. 12. Enoch Goodale. Aged, 89 years. He was once sexton to the Friends, Quakers. Married out of their communion; first, at 23, a Buxton with whom he lived thirty years, then a Bell, with whom he lived nine years. Three sons left; one only in the state, one in Maine, one in Conn.

1070. Apr. 12. Peter Frye. Dysentery, 60 years. Son of Col Frye, a British pensioner, and grandson of Col. B. Pickman. Thirty-seven years in Salem.

1071. May 30. Nicholas Lane, sailmaker. Cancer, 67 years. Employed every physician of whom he could hear. He from Cape Ann. Married first, at 22, Anna Bezoel, who died in 1809, and with whom he lived thirty-one years; second, widow Mary Buffum, with whom he lived thirteen years. Eleven children left, three sons and eight daughters. Derby street, between Carlton and Becket.

1072. June 16. Capt. George Crowninshield. Age, 81 years. He the grandson of an emigrant, Dr. J. C. R. C. from Leipsic. He married, at 23, a daughter of Richard Derby, esq., with whom he lived fifty-seven years. Six children left, four sons and two daughters. One son, George, and daughter, unmarried, in family with him. Father of Jacob, Member of Congress, and B. Secretary of the Navy. Very temperate and active till the last. Drank little but water for a month before death. Derby street, between Daniels and Orange, cor. of Orange.

1073. July 6. Edward, child of Nathaniel and widow Abigail Chever. Suddenly, 18 months. Complaint in the bowels, pink root administered, and almost instant death ensued. Physicians both young, etc. Father died in 1813, and left four children. She a Hutchinson (see Nov. of that year). Three children left, two males. Carlton street.

1074. July 6. John, son of John and Eunice Harwood. Suddenly, 31 months. As in the other case; complaint in the bowels, pink root administered, and almost instant death ensued. Same physicians. Buried a child in April, 1814. He is a prisoner taken from one of our U. S. vessels, the Syren. She a Ridgway, mother now a Bedney. Essex street above Pleasant.

1075. July 8. Sara, daughter of John and Sara Plantine. Atroph. inf., 6 years. She a Ward, died lately, a Baptist. He a foreigner. One male child left. Derby street, between Becket and English.

1076. July 27. Hanna Mansfield, maiden. Age, 80 years. Her mother was an ancient schoolmistress in east part of Salem for many years, died in 1791, æt. 82, and left only this daughter and a house for her in Derby street. Died at Fort Lee.

1077. July 29. George, child of George and Mary Wright. Mortification in bowels, 4 months. Fine child, good mother. Complaint not well understood. She a Cleaves, married in 1811. Mother a Scot. Father from Gothenburg in Sweden. Has been long absent at sea. One child, a son, left. Hardy street, below Derby.

1078. Sept. 10. Elizabeth Putnam, dau. of Edw. and Anna Allen. Dropsy in head (so said), 10 years. He abroad and separated from his family by his affairs. Son of late Capt. Edward Allen. She a daughter of the late Gen. John Fiske. Five children, two males and three females. E. Vine Street, south of Walnut, in Gen. Fiske's mansion.

1079. Sept. 21. Sara, widow of Charles Edey. Complication, 74 years. She was a Grey, married in 1768, at 26, and lived in married life thirteen years. Left two children, daughters.

1080. Sept. 23. John, child of John and Mercy Upton. Dysentery, 16 months. Only child. She a Townsend, dau. of Samuel Young. He, son of Mr. Upton on Pickman's farm.

1081. Sept. 27. Female child of Zechariah F. and Sarah Silsbee. Sore mouth and dysentery, 24 days. He a son of N. Silsbee and brother of N. and William. She a Boardman, mother a Hodges. Three children left, one female. Pleasant street, opp. Washington Square, west side.

1082. Sept. 28. John, of Samuel and Martha Silsbee. Abscess and consumption, 15 years. He a son of Samuel and Martha. Grandmother living, dau. of Deacon Prince. Mother a Read. Five children left, two sons. Daughter settled in Vermont, another in Boston. Webb street.

1083. Oct. 14. Mary, widow of Oliver Berry. Fever, 77 years. Not a week's illness. A meek woman, much regarded. She a Brown, married Jan. 1765, at 22, living three years in married life. No children survive, seven grandchildren. A widow fifty years and widow indeed. Essex, cor. of Turner street.

1084. Oct. 20. Widow Grace Hampson. Aged, 86 years. Born in Marblehead, lived in Salem twenty years. She was a Horn of Marblehead, married at 26 and lived ten years in married life. She left three children; one daughter Card, a son with whom she repeatedly lived in Salem, now removed to Boston, and a son in Maine. Was at board with her granddaughter Hayes in Salem. A sister, S. Fletcher, survives. English street, near Essex.

1085. Oct. 24. Nancy, wife of David Phippen. Fever, 37 years. Married at 21 and lived sixteen years in married life. Her mother a Cooke, grandfather a Clough. Six children left, four sons and two daughters. He a grandson of deacon D. Phippen. St. Peter street, below County.

1086. Nov. 4. John, of Samuel and Lydia Buffum. Convulsions, 9 months. She a daughter of Nicholas Lane who died in May. Four children left, two males. He belongs to Salem, removed to Charlestown and returned. Walnut street between W. and Elm.

1087. Nov. 7. Margaret, widow of Benjamin Nurse. Fever, etc., 67 years. She was a Welcome in Daniels street. Married at 26, and lived thirty years in married life. Her husband a baker. Left two children; eldest son in Boston. Her brother Thomas married a Lambert. A sister Foye only one left. Daniels street.

1088. Nov. 17. Elizabeth, wife of John Wells, aged 67. She was a Darling. Twice married; first at 21, a Talbot, with whom she lived six years, then a Wells, with whom she lived six years. No children by last marriage. Two children, sons, living in 1809.

1089. Nov. 17. Peter Green, African servant of Maj. Gen. N. Green, a hero of the Revolution. Aged, 80 years. Twice married; first, at 21, living in married life fourteen years, and second marriage of sixteen years. Born in Africa. Came to Salem after the war and married Flora Gerrish, who died four years ago. He was comfortable while she lived, then poor. Two children, son and daughter, not living in Salem.

1090. Nov. 26. Mehitable, wife of Michael O'Brian. Fever, 50 years. She was a daughter of Capt. John Harthorne and married first, at 18, a King, with whom she lived two years; second, in 1786, Samuel Giles, with whom she lived eighteen years, and by whom she had two children, males; third, her present husband, who was from Ireland, married in Boston. Derby street near Union.

1091. Dec. 19. Robert, child of William and Sara Bates. Eruptive fever, supposed measles, 15 months. Mother a sister of Charles Forbes. Northey street.

DEATHS IN 1816.

1092. Jan. 2. Jacob Haynes from Prussia. Consumption, 52 years. A seaman. Married, first, a widow Webb and had a daughter-in-law. She died Sept. 21,

1808, æt. 49, from Wilmington, N. C.; second, at 40 years of age, the present wife, with whom he lived four years. No children by last wife. Derby, near Daniels street.

1093. Jan. 6. Gideon Woodberry, from Beverly. Consumption, 58 years. Eleven children remain of four marriages. Winter street, King's house between Bridge and Pickman streets.

1094. Jan. 7. Note of the death of Salmon Goodrich, captain. Fever abroad, 45 years. Said to have died on his passage from New Orleans to New York, as by merchant's letter. Went from Salem to coast from New Orleans to southern ports, leaving Salem last March. He came from Berlin. Connections. Resided six years in Salem. Married Mary Dutch of Ipswich. Four children left, all females. Becket street.

1095. Jan. 7. Note of the death of William, son of Samuel and Mary Masury. Lost at sea, 17 years. Sailed for France in the sch. Diligence, belonging to Stone & Co., Nov. 10, 1812. Third son. She has five children left, one daughter. Two sons at sea. Hardy street.

1096. Jan. 14. John Dawson, mariner, of Guernsey Island. Aged, 86 years. At 32, he married Sara White, widow Whittemore, by whom he had two children, a son and daughter, and with whom he lived fifty-three years. She was first married at 18, living six years with her first husband, and had by him one child. At 25, she married Dawson, and is now living, aged 77 years. He had escaped seven times from men-of-war impressed. In 1757 was taken by Indians at Crown Point. Was five years in British ships after marriage.

1097. Jan. 15. Alexander, son of Daniel and Mehitable Knight. Cynanche trachealis, 3 years. He from

Haverhill, she a Gardner. This child and one in an adjoining tenement, of one Carter of same age, taken together and died together, about two days.

1098. Jan. 29. Elizabeth, wife of Joseph Deland. Asthma, 62 years. She was a Cox. Married, first, at 19, a Robbins with whom she lived three years, and by whom she had one child; married second, a Willick with whom she lived seven years, and had three children; third husband twenty years, and by him one child, all dead. He a son of Joseph Deland, former wife a Bacon, by whom he had children. He holds property from his father for his children.

1099. Feb. 18. Abiel, widow of Ebenezer Tozzer. Aged, 88 years. She married in 1750, at 22, and lived in married life twenty years. Left one daughter Mary, who served her, and one son. Her mother Whitefoot died in 1790, æt. 103 years. Orange street below Hodges.

1100. Mar. 2. News of the death of Capt. John Becket. Abroad at sea, 40 years. He went to the southward, to sail from Norfolk, and died on his passage to Cork, Ireland. He married, at 31, Sara, dau. of deacon James Browne, living nine years in married life. He, son of John, of the Committee, who died in 1804, æt. 58. They have three children, two males. Derby street, between Becket and English.

1101. Mar. 14. Male child of Henry and Hanna E. Allen. Atroph. inf., 2 weeks. He was the youngest son of Capt. Edw. Allen and she a dau. of Capt. William Allen. The father is now missing. Two children left. The family lives in the same house with the family of Capt. J. Becket. Derby street between Becket and English.

1102. Mar. 24. Thomas Masury, son of Thomas and

Mercy. Consumption, etc., 56 years. This name is almost extinct among us. The adults are gone and their families in first generation. They held considerable property, now none. He married in 1788, at 29, Lydia Swasey, who died in 1808. Three sons left. One settled at Chebacco, married.

1103. May 6. George, of George and Elizabeth Hodges. Fever, 3 years and 4 months. She a Welcome, dau. of Thomas. Mother, dau. of Capt. George Lambert. One child left. Hardy street, below Derby.

1104. May 6. Robert Richardson, house-carpenter. Consumption, 36 years. Married, at 31, a daughter of James Becket, with whom he lived five years. Left three children. Has lived in Salem fifteen years. He from Westford. Parents living and brothers and sisters. Becket street near Derby.

1105. May 6. Margaret, widow of Capt. Richard Valpy. Fever, 72 years. She was a Batcheler of Wenham, and married first, at 20, a Henly of Marblehead, with whom she lived twenty years in married life; second, in 1788, R. Valpy, with whom she lived eleven years. He married, first, Hanna Ives who died in 1756. He died in 1799, æt. 65. She has a brother and sisters at New Ipswich. Hardy street, near Essex.

1106. May 12. Mary, wife of Capt. John Peters. Consumption, 55 years. She was a dau. of Jonathan Archer. Married first, in 1784, at 22, Elisha Gunnison, with whom she lived five years, and had one son; second, in 1795, Jacob Norman, with whom she lived two years, and no child survives; third, in 1800, her present husband, living in married life sixteen years, and has one child left. Bridge street, Skerry's.

1107. May 19. Edmond Whittemore, house-carpenter. Found dead, 66 years. Married, at 24, Hanna

Pierce, who died last March, with whom he lived forty-two years. No children. His father, a house-carpenter, married second wife Sara Murray in 1756; she died in 1786, æt. 67.

1108. May 28. Mary Newton, dau. of John and Ruth Newton, 49 years.. Her father died before I came to Salem. Mother a Searle. Two sisters, Grant and Bartlet, living.

1109. May 30. Isaac Oakman, sailmaker and mariner. Infirm, 71 years. Apparently in a decline. Long lame from an injury in the knee by a fall. He married, first, at 24, a Bates of Lynn, with whom he lived twenty-two years and had two children, two sons. Many grandchildren remain. Married, second, a Swasey, widow Sullivan. Children not in Salem.

1110. May 31. Ann, of Jeremiah and Elizabeth O'Conner. Atroph. inf., 18 days. He from Ireland. She a Longeway and her mother a dau. of madam Rhue. They are Catholics. The grandmother lives in the English house next the gate. Her two daughters with her, both Longeway. Three children left, two males. Dalrymple's Building near old Neck Gate, Essex street.

1111. June 16. William Crispin, rigger. Injury from a blow, 62 years. Married, at 28, a Dawson with whom he lived thirty-four years. Left eight children, one son and seven daughters. The father William, in 1755, married Margaret Swasey. English street.

1112. June 17.. Male child of Robert and Sara Brookhouse. Soon after birth, 2 days. She a dau. of Jonathan Archer. Mother a Woodman. This their first child. Husband's father dead. Mother and children living. Both parents have large families. Northey street, below Bridge.

1113. June 23. John, of John and Elizabeth Cook.

Convulsions, 5 years. Child without appetite for several days. He a son of widow H. Keen of Patfield. Takes the name of John Cooke, but this is indeed his Christian name only. Two children left, son and daughter. Brown street, between Oliver and Fairfield, Common.

1114. June 24. Hannah, widow of Thomas Schetswell, 31 years. She was a dau. of Thomas and Hanna Rowell. Mother a Becket. Father from Ipswich. Married at 19 and lived five years in married life. Two children left, a son and daughter. Turner street, between Essex and Derby.

1115. July 3. Sara, wife of David Magoun, shipwright. Consumption, 38 years. Long infirm. She a Hitchins from Lynn, married at 24, and lived thirteen years in married life. Left five children, three daughters. Her father living with her. He from Pembroke. Becket street.

1116. July 7. William Rantoul, clerk of barque Camel, Breed. Scurvy, at sea, 22 years. Worthy youth. Died in our bay four days before getting in. Body lodged at the Hospital Ground. He kept the name of his mother's first husband. A brother and sisters at Beverly.

1117. July 13. Abigail of Abijah and Elizabeth Bartlet. Dropsy in the head, so said, 9 years. A very high fever. From Marblehead. Has three sons and one daughter, one daughter married. He a ropemaker. Union street, Brown House tenant.

1118. July 14. William Obear, mariner, 50 years. He married a Betsy Maservy late in life, a sister of Mr. John Osgood's wife. He has two sisters, Lambert and Hall. Buried from his brother Lambert's. Lived among his friends and relatives.

1119. July 17. Mary, widow of Robert Rantoul. Decay, 61 years. She was a Preston. Twice married.

First, at 19; time in marriage, nine years. Her son William died July 7. Robert Rantoul, Esq., is Rep. of Beverly, with whom she lived. Mary, widow Peabody. Left two children, son and daughter. Widow R's mother a Lambert. Had four children. Services at Beverly, but body transported to Salem for interment. Has a house in Essex street, Pleasant street, and a pew in East Meeting-house.

1120. Aug. 9. Hanna, wife of Bundeh Sabteh, a Malay, 38 years. She was a Whitefoot, thrice married, and left six children. Had two before she married the Malay. Of great muscular strength and corpulent. See D. B.

1121. Sept. 10. Hanna E., wife of Capt. Henry Allen. Palpitation of the heart, 25 years. She was a dau. of Capt. William Allen of Salem, from Manchester, and married at 19; time in marriage, six years. Left two children, son and daughter. Born at Manchester. He a son of Capt. Edward Allen, deceased. Was at New York preparing for a voyage. Had been cast away.

1122. Sept. News of the death of Capt. Abner Briggs at New Orleans. Fever, 31 years. He was a son of Johnson Briggs from Old Colony who settled in Salem before the Revolution. Married, at 30, a dau. of Rev. John Giles of Newburyport, who came from England a Presbyterian. Time in marriage, one year. Left one child, a son. Capt. Briggs had the kind care of Capt. R. Ward of Salem. Of schooner Cyrus from Salem. Three sons and three daughters of Johnson Briggs still live. Rev. Giles has two daughters and a son.

1123. Oct. 27. Debora, wife of Evsed Stoddart. Consumption, 51 years. She a Marsh, born in Hingham July 12, 1765. Married, at Hingham, July 14, 1782; time in marriage thirty-four years. Removed to Salem. She of the Baptist sect. A long time sick. Had ten children; six living, four sons and two daughters. Their son Eben born Jan. 11, 1787; drowned Dec. 7, 1807. Three children died young. Hardy street, between Derby and Essex.

1124. Nov. 14. Elizabeth, wife of Alexander Buchanan. Dropsy, 37 years. She a dau. of Nicholas Lane. Married first, in 1800, at 21, Josiah Gatchel, by whom she had two sons; time in marriage four years. Second, in 1805, A. Buchanan, an Englishman, supposed to be living; last seen on board of an English man-of-war. Time in second marriage, eleven years. One child by Buchanan. The three children at Ipswich, Wenham and Danvers. Nine children by N. Lane still live by three wives. Buried from W. Lane's, Turner, cor. of Derby street.

1125. Dec. 5. John Forbes, a seaman. Fever, 32 years. He married, at 19, Hepsibah House from Nantucket, and had three children, two sons. Time in marriage, thirteen years. John worked with a tallow-chandler and was a brother of Charles, now also a worthy man. The mother a Dawson and thrice married. First, a Forbes, and by him had three children; second, a Preston, by whom one child; third, a Whittemore, and by him one child. Essex, between Becket and Carlton streets.

1126. Dec. 12. Thomas Rowell. Instantly, 66 years. Born in Newburyport. Married, at 27, Elizabeth, dau. of William Becket, by whom he had six children, four sons and two daughters. Time in marriage thirty-nine years. He has no parents, brothers, nor sisters surviving. A very extraordinary family indeed. He was a boat-builder. Returned from work, supped, hummed a tune, smoked and died. Turner street, between Derby and Essex.

DEATHS IN 1817.

1127. Jan. 8. Susanna, of Henry Sauward. Aged, 78 years. She had been infirm. A woman of good endowments. She was a Batten and married first, in 1762, at 22, Josiah Beadle, by whom she had two daughters who survived her. The eldest married a Gwinn, the youngest, widow of John Dale. Lived with first husband thirteen years. Time in second marriage three years. Henry Sauward was from York, Me., and died in that part of the country. Turner street, between Derby and Essex.

1128. Feb. 12. Thomas King. Dropsy, 34 years. Came from New Brunswick, N. J., to Salem. Died in his chair while sitting at work. The first I buried from the new house.

1129. Feb. 24. Mary, of James and Hanna Standon. Atroph. inf., 3 weeks. Child appeared from birth very feeble. She a Perkins; he, at sea, a foreigner. One child left. Derby street, between Daniels and Hardy.

1130. Feb. 27. Sara Timothy, dau. of Jonathan and Mary Mason. Dropsy in head, 15 years. Named after the Timothys of So. Carolina. He died in 1808. First wife a King, who died in 1792 and left three children. One daughter lives, a Brooks. Second wife a King, five children, now two sons and two daughters. Vine street, between Elm and Liberty, Mason house.

1131. Mar. 4. William Peele, a cooper. Inflammation(?), rupture, etc., 79 years. Married Jan., 1762, at 24 years, Elizabeth Becket, dau. of John, by whom he had five children, all living; one son Robert and four daughters, two married, two widows. Time in marriage fifty-five years. Worthy man. Went to sea, but spent his life as here at his trade. His father a tailor in the centre of the town. Becket street on Becket's estate.

1132. Mar. 8. Mary, dau. of Capt. John Becket. Consumption, 27 years. She has suffered long, and very much for seven years. Her father died in 1804, her sister Elizabeth, who married a Waters, in 1809, at same age, and her brother John in 1816, news received in March. One child by first wife, son and daughter by second, none by third. She by Ingersoll, second wife. Becket's court near Becket street.

1133. Mar. 15. Sara, widow of Nathaniel Knight. Aged, 86 years. She a Mascoll, dau. of John and Sara, bapt. Jan. 23, 1732. Left a son Capt. N. Knight and two daughters Lethart and Ostrum. Lived with her son for many years in Deacon Prince's house, corner of Bath and Pleasant, old house. Her sister-in-law, Martha P., widow of S. Silsbee, born same year. Pleasant street.

1134. Mar. 17. Mary Tozzer, maiden dau. of Ebenezer and Abiel. Suddenly, 67 years. She has left a sister, and brother William and sister-in-law a Patterson, widow, married a Lane. Her mother died at 88 years of age, and her grandmother at 103. For thirty years, the deceased was the faithful companion of her mother. Orange street.

1135. Apr. 21. Susanna, of William Becket. Aged, 94 years. She was a Fowler of Ipswich. Family removed to Newmarket. Married, at 22, and lived sixteen years in married life. Lived a widow fifty-six years with her dau.-in-law. Had eight children, none living. Has many of her posterity in New England. Her sister, mother of wife of John Norris. See D. B. Husband ship carpenter. She died in Ash street. Most of life in east part of the town.

1136. Apr. 23. Hannah, dau. of Samuel and Mary Manning. Aged, 78 years. Richard Manning, esq., a brother and three sisters lived a long life together. This the last and they have left a great estate to the family of Hodges. Elizabeth died in 1801, æt. 72; Richard Manning, esq., in 1811, æt. 80; Margaret, in 1813, aged 79; Jacob in 1815, æt. 78. Their eldest sister Mary married John Hodges, in 1749. Essex street, between Curtis and Herbert.

1137. June. News of the death of George Shaw, in the care of John Hunt. At sea, 16 years. He was adopted by this worthy man and wife from her relations being without children. They educated him well and with good hopes. The ship had just left Java on the voyage homeward, taken sick and soon died. The first time at sea. Bath street, the house of J. Hunt.

1138. June. News of the death of Thomas Dean, son of John and Christiana Ward. Fever abroad, 17 years. At Matanzas, Cuba. It has been very sickly on these islands. Taken after landing, perhaps after eating fruit freely. The first time at sea. John, son of John. Christiana, dau. of Capt. Thom. Dean by his second wife a Cash. They have two children left, one son. The mother a woman of great ambition. Carlton street.

1139. June. News of the death of Nathaniel, son of Samuel and Rebecca Silsbee. Lost at sea, 23 years. Drowned Sept. 14, 1816, when six days from port. They have one son and three daughters left. Two married out of town. She a Patten. His mother a Prince living still. Webb street.

1140. July 6. Lydia, widow of Capt. Ebenezer Pierce. Dropsy, 77 years. She was a Brown, married at 25, and lived twenty years in married life. Her husband died at sea in 1784. Her sister Berry died from same house, at the same age, 77, Oct. 14, 1815. Two children left. Two children of son living, one missing, grandchildren, great-grandchildren and son's widow. Her daughter Odlin had the charge of her. Turner street.

1141. July 12. Female child of Samuel and Abigail Derby. From laudanum, 3 months. Administered through mistake. She a dau. of widow of Nicholas Lane by a former husband Buffum. Three children left, one son. Blaney street, below Essex and Becket.

1142. Aug. 10. Sara, widow of Capt. Timothy Welman. Apoplexy, 58 years. She a Wyatt, married at 18; time in marriage thirty-three years. She had been much of a domestic woman. Her father and mother died in 1796. W. Wyatt, the son, in 1794, and her husband Timothy in 1810. His father died, at 91, in 1787, mother in 1811 and Adam in 1786. Six children left, three males. Derby street between Daniels and Hardy.

1143. Aug. 13. Edward Gibaut, son of Robert and Rebecca Stone. Teething, 13 months. The child extremely thrifty, but the real disorder probably unknown. She a dau. of Capt. John Osgood, Brown street. He son of Robert Stone and Anstis Babbidge. Six children left. This the first they have lost. Essex street, Brown house, cor. of Walnut street.

1144. Aug. 18. Widow Lydia Alexander. Apoplexy, 78 years. She a Woodhull, dau. of wife of I. Babbidge. Married, first, at 17, a Lander, with whom she lived three years; time in second marriage six years. Daughter by last husband. One daughter married a Francis with seven children, six females. She had been a widow fifty years.

1145. Aug. 25. Capt. Robert Stone. Apoplexy, 73 years. Married, in 1772, at 28, Anstis Babbidge, dau.

of C. and Anstis Babbidge. Mother a Crowninshield. He of Benjamin and Elizabeth. He was a chairman of the committee of proprietors of East meeting-house. Taken on Thursday night. The affection was in the throat, and most powerful means employed. He ceased to speak or swallow on the next night and lay insensible until he expired, Monday, 10 A. M. Two children left, son and daughter. Daughter widow of And. Dunlap. Hardy street near the East meeting-house.

1146. Aug. 25. Mary Ann of William and Sara Bates. Atroph. inf., 14 months. She a dau. of John Forbes. Mother married a Whittemore. Husband abroad at sea. His father upon the theatre in Boston. Two children left, males. Essex, cor. of Pleasant street.

1147. Aug. 26. Ann Elizabeth of Capt. Richard and Lydia Ward. Inflammatory fever, 2 years, 9 months. The third daughter. She a Robinson of Lynn. He has just returned from New Orleans, intending to settle there. Her father has removed from Lynn to Boston. His father living and at the funeral. Carlton street.

1148. Sept. 1. Benjamin D., son of Benjamin and Elizabeth Chandler. Convulsions, 11 years. His mother a Dean. Father absent. Only child. Hardy street, near meeting-house.

1149. Sept. 8. Moses Gage, of Moses and Nancy Hobson. Atroph. inf., 15 months. Only child. He from Rowley, a carpenter. She a Masury, gr. dau. of Deacon W. Brown. Andrew street.

1150. Sept. 11. Abigail, widow of Nathaniel Rogers. St. Anthony's fire, 53 years. She a Dodge of Ipswich, married at 21, and lived fifteen years in married life. In adverse circumstances came to Salem, was a distinguished school-mistress and educated her children well. Four sons survive her in Salem, Nathaniel, John, Richard and

William. He a son of Rev. N. Rogers of Ipswich. Lynde street.

1151. Sept. 15. John Patterson. Fever, 35 years. A grandson of Deacon Webb. Married, at 21, Susanna Eulen, granddaughter of Capt. ; time in marriage fourteen years. Sick before he landed, reached home, seized with delirium and so expired. Left six children, one son. Derby street.

1152. Sept. 15. Elizabeth, dau. of Zachariah and Sara Silsbee. Atroph. inf., 9 mos. He a son of Capt. N. Silsbee, and brother of Nathaniel, Member of Congress, and of William. She a dau. of Capt. F. Boardman, and sister of Mary Crowninshield, wife of B., Secretary of the Navy. Pleasant street, east gate of Washington Square.

1153. Sept. 15. Martha, widow of Samuel Silsbee. Aged, 86 years. She a dau. of John, son of Deacon Richard Prince, married at 24, and lived forty-seven years in marriage. A pleasant, faithful and worthy woman. Very active for her years until near the close of life. Her husband died Dec. 1803, æt. 73. Left three children, one son, daughter a Sage, and Read. Daniels street in Daniels' house, corner upon Essex street, near meetinghouse.

1154. Sept. 24. Joseph, son of Joseph and Sara Newell. Atroph. inf., 4 years 4 months. The child from a full habit became emaciated in a short time. Physicians explained nothing. She a Dunckley. They have three children, one male. Essex street between Becket street and court.

1155. Oct. 8. Male child of Judah and Eliza Dodge Atroph. inf., 6 days. She a Perveare of Hampton Falls and a relative of Edward of Boston. Her family from Isle of Jersey. His trade a mason. They have lost many children young. She a very healthy woman, he more feeble. Three children left, one son. English street.

1156. Oct. 8. David of John and Sara Becket. Fever, atroph., 23 months. The child long sick and fever upon fever. Father died at sea. (See Mar. 2, 1816.) She a daughter of Deacon James Browne by Masury. Two children left, one male. Brown street on Pleasant street.

1157. Oct. 9. Male child of John C. and Priscilla Clemens. Fever, etc., 6 months. She a Burroughs and has four children living, one son. He, by a former wife Bright, three, one son. They belong not to this part of the town and have moved to the last house, formerly Perkins' on Manning's lot. Belongs to the Branch. Essex street, near Neck Gate.

1158. Oct. 21. Mary of John and Jane Stickney. Dropsy, 24 years. Father from Newburyport. Mother a Chapman from Newbury. Eight children left, six males, two females. Family unknown to me till this event. Webb street.

1159. Oct. 23. Francis, of Jeremiah and Elizabeth O'Connor. Fever, 4 years. Catholics living among us. A female child of same parents burned in May, 1816. He from Ireland. She a Longeway. Two children left, one male. Dalrymple's B. near old Neck Gate. Essex, opp. English street.

1160. Oct. 25. Samuel, son of Samuel and Lydia Leach. Fever, 20 years. Both his grandmothers living. Mother, dau. of W. Becket. Four children left, two males. Turner street, below Derby.

1161. Oct. 30. Male child of William and Elizabeth Crispin. At birth. He of Salem. They have one male child left. St. Peter's street, below Church.

1162. Nov. 1. Male child of Benjamin and Mary

Blanchard. Atrophy, 1 year. He from Woburn, formerly a butcher. Has been troubled with rheumatism and lost the best use of one hand. She from Beverly, an Adams, second wife. They have eight children left, five sons. Dalrymple's Building, Essex street, opp. English.

1163. Nov. 26. Capt. George Crowninshield. Angina pectoris, 51 years. He returned in the Cleopatra, Oct. 3. Was soon after afflicted in the breast, complained to his friend, died on the barque at Crowninshield's wharf in the arms of his servant Hanson. Six brothers began life together and this is the third of the six departed. For their history, see No. 3669, 53, 317.

1164. Dec. 2. John Ward, formerly master of a vessel, shipkeeper. Drowned, 51 years. He was attending a vessel on W. side of Crowninshield's wharf; was found with his lantern on east side, not accounted for. Son of John and Bethia; married, at 29, Christiana, dau. of Capt. Thomas Dean, living in married life twenty-two years. His father died in 1789. Grandfather kept the tavern of Lynn, Old Road. Lost a son in June, 1816. One son and daughter left. Carlton street.

1165. Dec. 11. Female child of Francis and Elizabeth Goss. Atroph. inf., 14 months. Child long sick. She a dau. of James Becket. His father Thomas Goss, a Spaniard. Came young to America. One child left, male. Father a mariner. Near Universal meeting-house, Rust street.

DEATHS IN 1818.

1166. Jan. 13. Susanna, wife of Capt. Benjamin Dean, mariner. Fever, 71 years. She was a dau. of James and Mary Collins, married at 23, and lived forty-eight years in marriage. Baptized in 1747. Mother a Becket, dau. of John. He a brother of late Capt. Thomas

Dean. Two daughters married, one a Hunt, another a Chandler. Four children left. Old Dean House, Hardy street, near meeting-house.

1167. Feb. 10. William Greaves, from Ireland. Consumption, 35 years. Catholic. Died in the Charity House after a short time. Came to Massachusetts Sept. 22, 1816 and to Salem Aug. 11, 1817, from Demerary, a stranger.

1168. Feb. 13. Mary, widow of Deacon William Browne. Suddenly, 78 years. She was a Collins, married in Marblehead. First husband an Orne. Time in second marriage five years. She lived in the family of Rev. W. Whitwell. Was a woman of cheerful temperament and excellent disposition. Was on a visit in Marblehead. Buried in Salem in the family tomb. Deacon Browne died in 1811. Curtis street.

1169. Feb. 23. Thomas G. Day. Suddenly, 38 years. Married, at 37, a Benyon with three children. Time in marriage five months. He had a complaint like angina pectoris. Was at his work three days before he died. Had been in America several years. Had parents, brethren and sisters in Ireland. Daniels street near Derby.

1170. Mar. 25. Jacob, of Richard and Ann Crowninshield. Atrophy, 13 months. She from Ireland, he a son of George Crowninshield of Salem. Child died at the farm in Danvers, first Epes, then Derby, then Crowninshield & sons. One mile above the lower meeting-house. They have eight children left, four males.

1171. Mar. 30. News of the death of Andrew Palfray at Smyrna. Small pox, 23 years. Son of Mr. Richard Palfray, late of Salem. Three sons of Richard Palfray left and one daughter Nancy. The sister Nancy widow Pierce and lives in the Mansion House. Two brothers abroad. Derby street, H. of Blaney street, near Becket.

1172. Apr. 10. News of the death of Nathaniel Richardson, son of Nathaniel and Eunice, at Malaga, Spain, Jan. 21. Fever, 48 years. Of good natural powers. Deaf in youth. Had been unsuccessful in business, and had at last established himself in Malaga, Spain.

1173. April 27. Abigail, widow of Capt. Edward Gibaut. Aged, 74 years. She was a Yell and was second wife to Capt. E. G. She had been brought up in Capt. G's family and lived in the family when his first wife died and was much esteemed. Her first husband a Whittemore. His first wife Sara Crowninshield. Time in second marriage eight years. Capt. Gibaut died in 1803, æt. 75. Andrew street.

1174. May 7. Nancy, widow of Nathaniel Brown. Dropsy, 70 years. Married at 22, and lived eleven years in marriage. Her mother a Meservey, family name Welman. She has three sisters. One married Capt. John Osgood, another Obear, one single. She has been infirm for a long time. Lived and died at her son-in-law's W. Lane. Derby street, west side, east corner of upper Turner street.

1175. May 17. Ruth, widow of Francis Rust. Cramp in stomach, 78 years. She was sister of Richard Manning who died Apr. 19, 1812. Married at 58, lived in Ipswich and about the time of her brother's death removed into his family in Salem. Third wife to Francis Rust. Time in marriage five years. Was of retired life. Was in her chair when she died. Herbert street.

1176. May 17. Sara E. W. S., dau. of James W. and Lydia Stearns. Fever, 14 months. The child indisposed a short time. She an Emerson of Topsfield, gr. dau. of Rev'd Emerson of that place. Two children left, one son. Boston street.

1177. June 1. Frederick MacCormick, late from Ireland. Fever, 50 years. He was a Catholic, but in person to me unknown. He had no kindred near him and became one of the state poor, and died in our Charity House.

1178. June 5. Male child of Benjamin and Mary Patterson. Atroph. inf., 9 months. She a dau. of Major Barnes. He long sick and in decline, a son of my worthy friend W. Patterson. Mansion house of his father. Not blessed in his children. Herbert street.

1179. June 17. William Dunn, cordwainer, from Ireland. Consumption, 35 years. He had not long since arrived, and had been employed in N. H. Penitentiary to teach his art. Was invited from Portsmouth to Salem to work at his trade. He soon found his condition, put himself under public charity and died in a few days.

1180. June 17. Isaac Williams, from New York, of African parents. Consumption, 23 years. Was spoken well of, while here. Had lately come to Salem and was among the State's poor, when sick.

1181. June 19. Richard, son of Samuel and Anna Masury. Consumption, 20 years. She a dau. of Deacon W. Brown. The father died in April, 1805, æt. 40, and left five children, two sons; now one son and three daughters remain. Two are married, Hobson and Sloacum. Andrew street.

1182. June 24. Child of Jeremy and Elizabeth O'Connor. Atrophy, 3 weeks. She a granddaughter of the aged Mrs. Rhue, neutral French, æt. 90. Buried a child 23 October last. Essex street near old Neck Gate, Dalrymple's Buildings.

1183. June 25. Benjamin Blanchard from Woburn. Apoplexy, 59 years. He had been in better circumstances. Had been at hard labor on the day before. (See Nov. 1 last.) Twice married; second wife dau. of Capt. Adams of Beverly. Left seven children. Essex street near old Neck Gate, Dalrymple's Buildings.

1184. June 27. Nathaniel Langley, at the Hospital. Consumption, 37 years. Just returned from sea, sick, and died soon after landing. Wife named Fanny. Married at 25 and lived twelve years in marriage. Wife and five children in Salem, not long resident.

1185. July 8. Capt. Benjamin Patterson. Consumption, 41 years. Was taken with bleeding at the lungs last April. Was the only surviving child of my friend Capt. W. Patterson. Married, at 22, a Barnes. Time in marriage fifteen years. Left four children, two sons and two daughters. Herbert street.

1186. July 24. John of John and Sara Becket. Worms, 5 years. She a Brown, dau. of James. Mother a Masury. One child left, a daughter. Brown street, corner of Pleasant, N. E. of the Common.

1187. July 28. Lucy, widow of Larrabee. Obstruction, 44 years. She was a Bickford, married at 20 and lived nine years in married life. Was in the family of A. Donaldson who married a Peele and they supported her during a long sickness; confined ten months. Sister married a Knapp. Left one child, a daughter. Becket street.

1188. Aug. 1. Mary, wife of Capt. William Ropes. Dropsy, 57 years. She was a dau. of Deacon W. Brown by his first wife Mercy White, married in 1755. Col. W. Ropes her son. She married, at 19, and lived thirty-eight years in married life. A worthy woman. Left three sons and five daughters. Curtis street.

1189. Aug. 18. William Southward, son of George and Abigail. Complication, 28 years. Long sick. Father and mother survive him. His mother a Foot, dau. of Pasca F. Five children left to them, three sons and two daughters. Essex street, between Turner and Carlton.

1190. Aug. 25. Sara, widow of George Leach.

Dropsy, 76 years. She a Trask of Beverly, married at 18, and lived twenty-three years in married life. Husband of Beverly, Captain. Has left two aged sisters, widows, Porter aged 78 and Hutchinson aged 74. The sisters have been very upright women. Two children left, one son Samuel, boatbuilder, and daughter, widow Waters. Church street, Hardy's house near Ship Tavern.

1191. Aug. 28. Sara, wife of William Lovelock. Consumption(?), 29 years. She a Day from Gloucester, and married first, at 18, a son of Major Rice of Portsmouth, by whom she had two children; time in first marriage six years, time in second marriage one year. Her father, mother and several sisters in Salem. Essex street, opp. East; house in the name of Joseph on the old Becket lot.

1192. Sept. 21. Frederick Francis, of Capt. William and Mary Allen. Dysentery, 2 years 4 months. He from Manchester. She a Palfray. They have built on the west part of the Hardy lot. Hardy below Derby.

1193. Sept. 21. Eliza Shedlock, dau. of Timothy and Sara Welman. Consumption, 17 years 9 months. Father and mother dead. Eldest brother lives in Maine, youngest sick at home. Two sisters remain. Derby street between Hardy and Daniels.

1194. Sept. 25. George, of George and Elizabeth Hodges. Dysentery, 8 months. He a son of George Hodges; wife a Welcome, and her mother a Lambert. One child left. Hardy street, below Derby, on Turner's lot.

1195. Sept. 26. News of the death of William Eulen, at sea. Fever, 33 years. Married, at 25, Mary Cooke, and lived eight years in married life. His mother dau. of Capt. John Battoon. Left three children, sons. The family live in the house of their father, near Crowninshield wharf.

1196. Oct. 11. Female child of William Babbidge. Atroph. inf., 18 months. He a son of Christopher Babbidge. She a dau. of M. and Mary Bateman, she a Batten. They have four children, one female. Turner street, on the Bateman estate.

1197. Oct. 15. Capt. John Allen, son of Capt. Edward Allen. Complication, 28 years. Married, at 21, Hanna, dau. of William Allen, with whom he lived six years. She died Sept. 10, 1816. Kindred by marriage. Two children left, one son and daughter. Was some time in Marine Hospital. Brought to Salem on the 9th of Oct. and died on the 12th. Norman street.

1198. Oct. 15. John Peters, son of Capt. John Peters. Lost at sea, 20 years. Left in the Albatross from Falkland Isles with oil, Aug. 30, lat. N. 34°, long. 50°. Washed overboard with captain, four saved, seven lost. The father from the Peters family of Essex. His second wife an Archer, first a Skerry. He lives on the Skerry estate, Bridge street.

1199. Oct. 21. Elizabeth White, of William and Elizabeth Carlton. Consumption, 19 years. An excellent young woman. Her grandfather brother to Hanna Carlton with whom I live. His first wife a Palfray. The granddaughter educated with her uncle White and named for her aunt White, a Stone. Essex street, above Newbury.

1200. Oct. 27. Mary Edward, dau. of Samuel and Lydia Leach. Throat, 10 years. The mother dau. of W. Becket. Grandmother, 90 years of age. He buried his mother last August, æt. 76. Their son Samuel buried Oct., 1817, æt. 20 years. Son and daughter living, very feeble. Turner street, below Derby.

1201. Nov. 17. Emma, wife of Daniel Blanchard. Consumption, 30 years. Married at 21 and lived nine years in married life. Her family name Saunders from Harvard, Mass. He from the interior. Four children left. Essex street, below Webb, in Brooks' building near Gate.

1202. Dec. 12. Susanna, wife of Walter Jeffrey. Fever, 52 years. Married at 22 and lived thirty years in marriage. Her mother Rebecca Smith was a Lovett of Beverly, widow of Samuel and died in 1795, æt. 63. Rebecca, a sister, married Thomas Williams in 1794 and died, æt. 25, in 1796, second wife. They have left four children, one son. He a son by W. Jeffrey who married a Hardy.

DEATHS IN 1819.

1203. Jan. 15. Francis Benson, skipper. Fever, etc., 65 years. Married at 22, and lived forty-three years in married life. Brother of Capt. Thomas Benson whose second wife married Henry Rust, Esq., and whose daughter married Capt. Robert Peele. Daughter settled at Attleborough, Mass., Gilmanton, N. H., and Kennebec, Me. One son at home, one abroad. He received a pension as Revolutionary soldier, of Salem. English street.

1204. Jan. 18. Mary, widow of Thomas Hutcheson. Rheumatic fever, 74 years. She was a Trask of Beverly, born there, married at 24, and lived twenty-two years in married life. Her husband died Aug. 28, 1786 and left seven children. Two daughters, Putnam and Chever, and a son, remain. Her sister Porter living in Salem. Turner below Derby.

1205. Jan. 23. George, son of George and Seeth Ropes. Consumption, 31 years. A painter. Deaf and dumb. Active, acute, circumspect and esteemed. Had a free use of signs and of his pen. His mother a widow, and a Millet. Father died at sea in 1807 and left nine children. Essex street, opp. Pleasant.

1206. Jan. 27. Hannah, wife of Thomas Kenny. Atrophy, 42 years. She born in Salem. Husband a foreigner, whether living unknown. Mother and sister in Danvers. Two children, one male.

1207. Mar. 1. George Gale, son of Capt. Noah Gale, bookbinder. Consumption, 25 years. Married, at 21, a Grazier from Ipswich, and lived four years in married life. He born in Maine. His mother a Dunham. His father from Plymouth. Her mother a Pulcifer. Two children left, one male. The father bought Capt. John Elkins' house of MacMellan and was lost at Block Island. His father's house, southeast corner of Turner street in Derby street.

1208. Mar. 13. Male child of Daniel and Jane M. Bickford. Atroph. inf., 4 weeks. He a brother's son of Capt. John Bickford. She a Trask, has no parents but a brother. Married in 1818 and removed to Charlestown. She returned, in his absence at sea, to Salem. Bridge street, west corner of Pleasant.

1209. Mar. 19. John Lane, mariner and sailmaker, son of Nicholas and Nancy. Consumption, 24 years. Long sick, appetite till last moment. Youngest son. He married, at 22, a dau. of Seth King, jeweller, who lived in Curtis street, and lived in marriage one year. Left one male child. Turner street, between Derby and Essex, in Goom's house from Portugal.

1210. Mar. 27. Sara, wife of Capt. William Fairfield. Bowels, 50 years. She was a Jowler, married at 32 and lived seventeen years in married life. Born in Marblehead, first house beyond Forrest River Mills. Came to Salem and lived with Jonathan Mason and then with Capt. E. Allen. No parents or collaterals. Allen street, between English and Webb.

1211. March. News of the death of Benjamin, son of Abijah Hitchins. At sea, 16 years. His first voyage. Father infirm, and child anxious to go to sea. Died in a few days after leaving Havana. Father married a Cloutman, whose mother was a Becket. Seven children, two sons and five daughters. Becket street.

1212. Apr. 6. Christopher Beals, shipjoiner from Boston, 51 years. Married first, at 21, Mary Downs with whom he lived six years, and by whom he had one child; second, a Bacon, who died Feb. 13, 1801, by whom one child and with whom he lived one year; third, Jan. 23, 1803, Nancy Crandall, dau. of Nicholas Lane, by whom three children, and with whom he lived sixteen years. She has three children living by Crandall. Lived last in English street.

1213. May 1. Male child of Benjamin and Mary Blanchard. Atrophy inf., 2 years. She from Beverly, an Adams. The father died June 25, 1817, from Woburn. After death of husband, she removed from Dalrymple's Building, Neck Gate, to Windmill Point. Three children, one male.

1214. May 17. Stephen, son of Stephen and Hanna Cloutman. Fever, 38 years. He had just returned from sea after the long absence of ten years. His lung fever continued seven days. At his sister Whipple's. His mother Hanna Smith. Seven children left of the family, three sons and four daughters. Derby house, or Derby street, between Union and Herbert.

1215. May 18. Mary, widow of Capt. Henry Elkins, 79 years. Enjoyed good health till near to death. Married at 20; time in marriage eleven years. Two children left. Son married Priscilla Mason; daughter married

Andrew Sleuman and Joseph Winn. Daughter has two children, son and daughter. Opposite East Meetinghouse in Essex street. Andrews house.

1216. May 18. James, son of James and Deborah Becket. Fever, 23 years. Sick in Batavia and on passage home. His mother from Bradford. Father son of William. Four sisters left. From his brother-in-law Kelly, near Universalist meeting-house.

1217. May 23. Joshua, son of John and Elizabeth Dodge. Fever. Child lately christened. The mother long feeble and father slender. She a Wait. Mother now widow Johnson. Three children left, one son. Essex street, between Dean and Shillaber. Mackay house.

1218. June 3. Sarah, widow of Jacob Stivers, sister of Maj. Gen. John Fiske. Fever, 70 years. She a dau. of Rev. Samuel Fiske of Salem, married at 22, not one year in married life. He was from Holland. Came to Salem from Boston; was a baker, and baked in Essex street above Elm, second lot. Opposite the pumps corner of Neptune and Vine streets, opp. Elm street.

1219. June 4. John Horne, mulatto, lately from sea. Fever, 31 years. He was born in Philadelphia, and came to this port about a fortnight since in a vessel belonging to Joseph Knapp. Charity House, entered as State poor.

1220. June 12. Elizabeth, wife of Capt. William Lane. Debility, 42 years. She was dau. of N. Browne, married at 19, and lived twenty-three years in married life. She was in youth a beautiful woman. Her mother Nancy Meservey. Her grandmother I know. A sister survives who married Capt. Timothy Welman. He son of Nicholas Lane. Mother died May, 1817, æt. 70. Three sons and five daughters survive. Derby street, corner of Turner.

1221. July 14. William Burroughs, seaman. Obstructions, etc., 23 years. Lived with his grandfather George Burroughs, an old pensionary soldier. Has a mother and sister living. Derby street, last lot on old neckway.

1222. July 16. John Dalrymple from Ireland. Debility, 47 years. Married, at 37, Rebecca Gardiner. His brother James was established in Salem as a watchmaker when John came. He afterwards removed to Portland and lately returned. Left a wife and two children. Essex street, corner of Herbert. Collins Hardy house.

1223. July 21. Martha, of James and Sara Dalrymple. Worms, 5 years. Not long sick, a pleasant child. He from Ireland, watchmaker. Holds tenements opposite English street, near old Neck Gate. She a dau. of Joseph Vincent, ropemaker. Have two children, females. Essex street.

1224. July 27. Martha, of Daniel and Mary Gilbert. Dysentery, 5 years. She was Mary Waters, married in 1806, and went to his home in Brookfield. She was upon a visit to her father with this very promising child which died in less than a week's illness. They have other children. Derby street.

1225. Aug. 9. John Carberry from Waterford, Ireland. Fever, 38 years. Came early from Ireland to Newfoundland, thence to Boston. He had been in Boston several years, as waiter in a store. Had been in Salem but a few weeks and delivered himself up to the Charity House.

1226. Aug. 13. Eunice Caroline, of Major Horatio and Harriet Perry. Convulsions, etc., 3 years. He from Pembroke. She a dau. of Capt. Nicholas Lane from Gloucester, but long of Salem. Three children left, one male. Carlton street.

1227. Aug. 24. John McKenzie, from Scotland. Fever, 75 years. Had been in Salem two years. Came to America before the American Revolution, and was in the land and sea service. He had lived with widow Child, sister of Dr. Stearns, and upon her retirement to her brother's family was induced to enter upon the poor's list of the state, hoping for a pension. A good character.

1228. Sept. 2. Female child of John and Elizabeth Cooke. Convulsions, 3 months. She a Patfield, dau. of Mrs. Mack. He of Salem, wounded pensioner. The child apparently well till day before its death. Dr. K. said a croup. Three children, two males. Williams street.

1229. Sept. 18. Capt. John Archer. Old age, 86 years. Married at 24 and lived fifty-seven years in married life. His wife a Beckford. His wife has been dead five years, a Norris. He formerly lived in Elm street, but removed to the house of his father, where he died. Six children left, four sons and two daughters. All his children but John married. River street, on North river.

1230. Sept. 21. Thomas Bagley, from Ireland. Drowned, 27 years. He was carrying off an anchor in high wind from Derby wharf, from sch. Hind. The boat upset. Buried from the Charity House on Wednesday, Sept. 22.

1231. Sept. 26. James, child of William and Rhue. Atrophy, 22 months. Hardy street, Diman house.

1232. Oct. 2. Male child of Horatio and Harriet Perry. Atrophy, 3 weeks. Child feeble from birth, mouth sore, etc. They lost a child in August last. He from Pembroke, she a dau. of Nicholas Lane. Three children left, one male. Carlton street.

1233. Oct. 5. Mary, wife of James Goomnūnsen.

Lethargy, 25 years. She was Mary K. Majore, dau. of John, married at 18, and lived seven years in married life. An only child. Her father, French, married Susanna Knight in 1793, who in 1807 married Francis Lamartine. Left one child. Turner street, between Derby and Essex.

1234. Nov. 16. Mary, widow of Michael Bateman. Debility, 53 years. She was a dau. of John Batton, married at 18, and lived thirty-five years in marriage. She kept a school; first her sight failed her, and then a general debility came on, palpitation, etc. Mother a Masury. Husband died lately in the hospital at New York. Left five children, two sons. One married in Rowley. Turner street.

1235. Dec. 26. John, of Thomas and Sara Haynes. Athophy, 6 weeks. Two children left, one son. Walnut street.

INDEX OF NAMES.

Abbot, 39, 110.
Abbott, 61, 110.
Abraham, 120.
Adams, 44, 45, 158, 161, 167.
Aden, 119.
Albree, 64.
Alexander, 30, 154.
Allen, 6, 7, 20, 40, 58, 60, 69, 73, 77, 78, 85, 86, 92, 93, 103, 106, 107, 112, 113, 115, 130, 132, 138, 141, 145, 149, 163, 164, 167.
Allyne, 45.
Andrew, 7, 28, 44, 74, 118, 121.
Andrews, 92.
Apmerp, 137.
Archer, 5, 8, 15, 16, 20, 25, 27, 32, 33, 35, 36, 37, 39, 41, 42, 47, 50, 53, 55, 56, 58, 63, 73, 74, 75, 76, 78, 79, 83, 85, 90, 91, 96, 98, 101, 109, 113, 116, 123, 137, 146, 147, 164, 170.
Ashbey, 59.
Ashby, 66, 87, 116, 117.
Ashley, 9.
Aubin, 110.

Babbidge, 19, 38, 49, 51, 53, 54, 74, 76, 81, 82, 83, 99, 100, 102, 112, 119, 123, 134, 154, 155, 164.
Backer, 54.
Bacon, 58, 145, 167.
Bagley, 170.
Bagnall, 38.
Balch, 44.
Bangs, 3.
Baptiste, 48.
Barker, 49, 78.
Barnes, 101, 105, 161, 162.
Barr, 83, 136, 137.
Bartlet, 34, 62, 95, 96, 147, 148.
Bartlett, 26, 42, 68, 74, 77, 78.
Bason, 20.
Basset, 5.
Batchelder, 61.
Batcheler, 146.
Bateman, 59, 127, 164, 171.
Bates, 32, 135, 143, 147, 155.
Baton, 66, 71, 86.
Batten, 59, 127, 151, 164.
Battern, 14.
Batton, 171.

Battoon, 80, 163.
Beadle, 18, 29, 115, 121, 151.
Beals, 58, 167.
Beans, 31.
Becket, 8, 9, 25, 27, 31, 34, 35, 36, 46, 48, 54, 55, 59, 63, 67, 72, 74, 75, 76, 79, 80, 83, 84, 89, 91, 95, 96, 103, 104, 106, 107, 111, 114, 115, 123, 126, 137, 138, 139, 145, 146, 148, 150, 151, 152, 157, 158, 162, 163, 164, 167, 168.
Beckford, 95, 100, 133, 170.
Bedney, 141.
Bell, 139.
Benson, 79, 88, 104, 165.
Bentley, 28.
Benyon, 159.
Berry, 17, 27, 33, 36, 62, 120, 136, 142, 153.
Best, 31.
Beverley, 18.
Bezoel, 140.
Bezoill, 52.
Bickford, 68, 113, 135, 162, 166.
Bishop, 82, 98.
Black, 101, 126.
Blanchard, 158, 161, 164, 167.
Boardman, 14, 16, 17, 45, 100, 122, 141, 156.
Bonnemaison, 65.
Bowden, 95.
Bowditch, 14, 19, 24, 28, 42, 45.
Boyd, 71.
Boynall, 122.
Branigan, 121.
Bray, 32, 47, 80, 103, 106.
Breed, 148.
Briers, 5.
Briggs, 17, 21, 22, 56, 66, 108, 109, 149.
Bright, 157.
Brookhouse, 147.
Brooks, 91, 151, 165.
Brown, 4, 5, 8, 10, 31, 48, 79, 90, 103, 104, 114, 115, 117, 124, 126, 132, 136, 142, 153, 155, 160, 161, 162.
Browne, 1, 12, 22, 34, 43, 56, 63, 69, 71, 72, 81, 83, 84, 89, 91, 94, 102, 112, 115, 117, 118, 123, 124, 128, 130, 145, 157, 159, 168.
Buchanan, 104, 150.

Buffum, 140, 142, 154.
Bulfinch, 137.
Bullock, 82, 84, 90, 102, 104, 112.
Burdett, 132.
Burke, 13, 65.
Burns, 17.
Burrill, 11, 28, 56, 77, 80, 92, 96, 124, 125.
Burroughs, 21, 43, 157, 169.
Bush, 38, 122.
Bushnel, 1.
Butler, 27.
Butman, 63, 66, 73.
Buxton, 89, 139.
Byrne, 17, 25, 42, 72, 97, 109, 139.
Byrnes, 31.

Caban, 64, 107.
Caldwell, 55.
Calley, 119.
Caln, 110.
Cane, 44, 45.
Carberry, 169.
Card, 142.
Carleton, 15.
Carlton, 64, 70, 83, 86, 89, 90, 118, 123, 124, 137, 164.
Carnes, 35.
Carr, 59.
Carrol, 2, 113.
Carroll, 55, 57, 81, 83, 87.
Carter, 145.
Cash, 21, 153.
Cashew, 12.
Center, 61.
Chandler, 155, 159.
Chapman, 109, 120, 157.
Chevalier, 53.
Chever, 4, 17, 19, 23, 27, 34, 60, 61, 87, 88, 90, 100, 102, 105, 127, 128, 129, 130, 133, 134, 140, 165.
Child, 170.
Chipman, 8, 11, 22, 32, 54, 59.
Choate, 97.
Chubb, 45, 50.
Churd, 38.
Clark, 2, 4, 10, 68.
Clarke, 41, 47.
Clary, 29.
Clearage, 64, 111.
Cleaves, 141.
Clemens, 77, 157.
Clifford, 92, 96.

(173)

INDEX OF NAMES.

Clift, 114.
Clough, 39, 59, 142.
Cloutman, 2, 3, 9, 10, 19, 36, 49, 56, 57, 76, 79, 87, 104, 167.
Cody, 68.
Coffin, 28, 34, 124.
Coffrin, 69.
Colan, 138.
Cole, 70, 114.
Collins, 10, 11, 16, 19, 22, 24, 26, 37, 41, 46, 48, 49, 51, 52, 55, 61, 63, 65, 67, 88, 93, 94, 95, 98, 108, 114. . 119, 120, 124, 137, 158, 159.
Cook, 90, 147.
Cooke, 4, 64, 70, 79, 90, 142, 148, 163, 170.
Coombs, 16.
Cooper, 65.
Cordwell, 85.
Cotel, 130.
Cotton, 11, 12, 14, 15, 100, 114, 119, 120, 123, 188.
Cowen, 133.
Cox, 4, 18, 44, 45, 54, 67, 80, 82, 97, 102, 114, 120, 145.
Crandall, 57, 167.
Crane, 23.
Creely, 103.
Crelly, 39, 77.
Cressy, 115, 116.
Crispin, 37, 84, 91, 97, 104, 113, 128, 147, 157.
Crookshanks, 23, 108.
Croswell, 131.
Crowninshield, 2, 19, 20, 22, 25, 54, 62, 68, 76, 77, 79, 93, 97, 99, 103, 105, 107, 112, 122, 126, 128, 130, 135, 139, 140, 155, 156, 158, 159, 160.
Curtis, 56, 111, 124, 138.

Dale, 27, 151.
Dalrymple, 147, 157, 158, 161, 167, 169.
Dane, 38, 77.
Daniel, 136.
Daniels, 43, 76.
Darling, 143.
Davis, 98.
Davison, 124.
Dawson, 91, 104, 113, 144, 147, 150.
Day, 159, 163.
Dean, 3, 6, 7, 10, 12, 14, 16, 17, 21. 26, 35, 60, 70, 78, 84, 89, 95, 119, 122, 132, 153, 155, 158, 159.
Deighton, 78.
Deland, 145.
Delano, 113.
Derby, 12, 15, 35, 40, 47, 48, 49, 52, 86, 100, 117, 131, 140, 154, 159.
Devereux, 62, 66, 85, 126.
Diamond, 48, 100.
Dighton, 10.
Dileton, 126.
Diman, 6, 7, 19, 29, 76, 106, 170.
Dimon, 59, 62.

Dixey, 138.
Dodd, 25, 66, 111.
Dodge, 12, 41, 61, 125, 132, 155, 156, 168.
Dolbeare, 32.
Donaldson, 85, 162.
Dorrel. 52.
Dorrell, 80.
Downs, 167.
Driver, 80, 119.
Dunckley, 156.
Dunckly, 113.
Dunham, 166.
Dunlap, 27, 42, 99, 139, 155.
Dunn, 161.
Dupy, 67.
Dutch, 120, 144.
Dwire, 43.
Dyer, 43.
Dyseton, 112.
Dystill, 112.

Eastey, 6.
Edey. 41, 47, 50, 128, 141.
Edget, 46.
Edwards, 47, 71, 92, 99, 106.
Eliot, 62.
Elkins, 6, 14, 18, 25, 44, 58, 139, 166, 167.
Ellingwood, 65, 127.
Ellison, 84, 103, 106.
Elwyn, 91.
Emerson, 79, 160.
Emerton, 69, 71, 74, 82, 96.
Endicott, 47, 109.
English, 1, 18. 37, 51, 72, 73, 74, 93. 122, 126, 129, 135.
Epes, 159.
Eulen, 75, 102, 156, 163.
Eustis, 101.
Evoy, 28, 48, 51, 122.

Fairfield, 8, 13, 16, 50, 52, 56, 67, 70, 71, 75, 110, 114, 123, 128, 131, 166.
Farmer, 118.
Farnum, 136.
Felt. 72.
Ferguson. 5.
Fisk, 37, 41.
Fiske, 1, 2, 18, 58, 62, 71, 99, 106, 141, 168.
Fitz, 6.
Flag. 55.
Fletcher, 110, 142.
Flint, 35, 49, 63, 74.
Fogg, 81.
Foot, 16, 54, 75, 76, 111, 132, 162.
Foote, 64, 77.
Forbes, 15, 44, 143, 150, 155.
Foster, 1, 30, 50, 57, 85, 101.
Fowle, 20.
Fowler, 152.
Foye, 22, 50, 93, 108, 119, 143.
Francis, 154.
Francks, 109.
Franks, 71, 121.
Freeman, 15.

French, 13, 63, 66, 79, 95, 171.
Frost, 22.
Fry, 13, 79.
Frye, 36, 140.
Furber, 88.
Furlong, 46.

Gaines, 32, 110.
Gale, 3, 22, 32, 68, 95, 96, 97, 115, 126, 127, 166.
Gales. 5.
Galloway, 138.
Ganson, 89, 124.
Gardiner, 36, 38, 63, 76, 169.
Gardner, 5, 29, 44, 78, 100, 105. 118, 119. 121, 132, 135.
Gatchel, 78, 89, 94, 150.
Gatchell. 58.
Gavett, 66.
Gayton, 44, 54.
Geering, 57.
Gerard, 135.
Gerrish. 143.
Gerry, 41.
Getchel, 104.
Gibaut, 20, 160.
Gilbert, 169.
Giles, 143, 149.
Gill, 91, 139.
Gilman, 55.
Gilmore. 46.
Goldsmith, 85, 133.
Goodale, 139.
Goodhue, 82.
Goodrich, 110, 114, 120, 131, 144.
Goom, 166.
Goomnünsen, 170.
Gordon, 41.
Goss, 75. 102, 158.
Gotier, 110.
Gowing, 94.
Grant, 7, 12, 13, 16, 43, 45, 47, 76, 147.
Graves, 101.
Gray, 56, 71, 94, 135.
Grazier, 166.
Greaves, 159.
Green, 55, 73, 88, 143.
Greenleaf. 134.
Greves, 126.
Grey, 115, 116, 141.
Groves, 102.
Guillen, 128.
Guillon, 134.
Gunnerson, 2, 3, 109.
Gunnison, 3, 9, 11, 39, 56, 146.
Gunter, 45.
Gwinn, 151.
Gyllingham, 21.

Hagar, 65.
Hall, 148.
Hamatt, 110.
Hammond, 137.
Hampson, 62, 142.
Hancock, 136.
Hannon, 43.
Hans, 136.
Hanson, 158.

INDEX OF NAMES.

Hardigan, 121.
Hardy, 115, 163, 165, 169.
Harrington, 2, 56.
Hart, 83.
Harthorne, 131, 132, 143.
Harwood, 134, 140.
Haseltine, 105.
Haskell, 70.
Hathorne, 55, 58, 72, 84.
Haven, 109, 120.
Hawkins, 47.
Hawthorne, 2.
Hayes, 108, 142.
Haynes, 143, 171.
Heald, 39.
Heard, 69, 71, 86.
Helmes, 83.
Henderson, 23, 118.
Henly, 146.
Herrick, 51, 70.
Hill, 8, 9, 23, 41, 78, 81, 85, 86, 92, 104, 112, 133.
Hiller, 36.
Hilliard, 9, 13.
Hitchborn, 85.
Hitchins, 6, 36, 76, 88, 89, 100, 113, 121, 148, 167.
Hobbes, 108, 109.
Hobson, 155, 161.
Hodgden, 38.
Hodges, 1, 5, 13, 14, 17, 18, 21, 23, 27, 32, 39, 42, 44, 50, 61, 71, 78, 83, 93, 107, 126, 132, 137, 141, 145, 146, 153, 163.
Hollet, 94.
Hollingworth, 72.
Holmes, 128.
Holt, 22, 31, 108.
Hooper, 97, 138.
Horn, 142.
Horne, 168.
Horton, 12, 43, 138.
Hosmer, 28, 50, 105.
House, 150.
Hovey, 42.
Howard, 132.
Howe, 117.
Hubbard, 75.
Hull, 127.
Hunt, 16, 73, 83, 92, 101, 153, 159.
Hutcheson, 3, 165.
Hutchinson, 55, 88, 89, 97, 113, 127, 130, 140, 163.

Ingersoll, 14, 17, 36, 40, 59, 72, 84, 111, 122, 137, 152.
Ives, 22, 72, 78, 146.

Jacobs, 13.
Jeans, 68.
Jefferds, 88.
Jeffrey, 165.
Jeffry, 12, 17, 27.
Jenkins, 79, 111.
Johnson, 64, 65, 70, 103, 108, 128, 134, 168.
Jowler, 166.

Kane, 119.
Karn, 110.

Keen, 17, 28, 68, 148.
Keene, 1, 2.
Kehew, 138.
Kehou, 12, 32.
Kelly, 168.
Kenny, 88, 92, 130, 166.
Kilby, 86.
Kimball, 8, 75.
King, 6, 17, 40, 52, 78, 83, 93, 106, 120, 126, 137, 139, 143, 144, 151, 166.
Kinsman, 61.
Kittridge, 90.
Knap, 8, 79, 126.
Knapp, 57, 65, 97, 125, 139, 162, 168.
Knight, 10, 18, 94, 144, 152, 171.
Knights, 24, 42, 58.
Knowlton, 6, 87.

Lamartine, 171.
Lambert, 1, 8, 11, 21, 29, 31, 33, 43, 44, 45, 52, 64, 70, 72, 73, 75, 80, 85, 88, 98, 117, 118, 128, 143, 146, 148, 149, 163.
Lander, 12, 20, 66, 86, 137, 154.
Lane, 52, 57, 76, 78, 89, 104, 111, 113, 117, 136, 140, 142, 150, 152, 154, 160, 166, 167, 168, 169, 170.
Lang, 111.
Langley, 162.
Lapature, 128.
Larabee, 121.
Laralle, 126.
Larrabee, 56, 138, 162.
Laskin, 33.
Lassell, 37.
Lawrence, 137.
Lazell, 97.
Leach, 2, 19, 34, 107, 157, 162, 164.
Leavitt, 5.
Ledbetter, 93, 108, 119.
Lee, 25, 37, 41.
Lefavre, 46, 117.
Legro, 40.
Leslie, 33.
Lethart, 152.
Lewis, 43, 62.
Lister, 123.
Little, 106, 121.
Lockart, 78, 132.
Lockhart, 93, 107.
Logan, 20.
Longaway, 101.
Longeway, 97, 111, 147, 157.
Lord, 20, 123, 128.
Loring, 15.
Lovelock, 163.
Lovett, 25, 165.
Lufkin, 64, 69, 112.
Lufkins, 46.
Lynde, 87.

Mac, 9.
Mac Cormick, 160.
Macdaniel, 68.
Macdonald, 31, 80.

Macewen, 60.
Mac Gregory, 20, 23.
Mack, 46, 170.
Mackay, 168.
Mackey, 135.
Macmellan, 104, 166.
Magoun, 76, 136, 148.
Majore, 171.
Malcom, 35.
Maley, 62.
Manning, 31, 50, 58, 113, 118, 128, 129, 134, 139, 152, 153, 157, 160.
Mansfield, 7, 13, 44, 119, 133, 141.
March, 82.
Marsh, 6, 64, 149.
Marston, 20, 33, 74, 76, 79.
Martin, 24, 28, 29, 42, 68, 101.
Mascoll, 53, 69, 75, 88, 111, 112, 130, 152.
Maservey, 128.
Maservy, 148.
Mason, 5, 14, 16, 17, 51, 52, 53, 54, 106, 151, 166, 167.
Massey, 132.
Masury, 2, 3, 5, 7, 22, 23, 28, 30, 31, 35, 37, 38, 39, 40, 42, 43, 51, 63, 65, 66, 86, 89, 90, 99, 107, 112, 114, 115, 118, 120, 122, 125, 126, 144, 145, 155, 157, 161, 162, 171.
Matisnon, 117.
Matthews, 40.
Mayberry, 24, 51.
McEwen, 90, 103.
McGowen, 95.
McGrew, 19.
McIntire, 81.
McKenzie, 170.
Mc'Rhue, 97.
Merriam, 86.
Meservey, 91, 160, 168.
Miller, 61, 62.
Millet, 25, 35, 43, 45, 47, 50, 54, 75, 80, 82, 85, 86, 91, 100, 115, 116, 119, 126, 137, 166.
Millett, 101.
Molloy, 77.
More, 47, 126.
Morgan, 119, 132.
Moritz, 114.
Moses, 4, 17, 129, 135.
Moulton, 38.
Muchmore, 52.
Mugford, 55, 56.
Munnion, 106.
Munyon, 94.
Murray, 6, 7, 11, 16, 21, 26, 34, 39, 41, 43, 56, 67, 68, 96, 99, 112, 133, 137, 147.

Nesboth, 12, 13, 15.
Newell, 82, 83, 108, 156.
Newhall, 1, 7, 23, 26, 29, 30, 113.
Newman, 94.
Newton, 23, 41, 147.
Nichols, 65, 88, 137.
Nicholson, 132.

176 INDEX OF NAMES.

Nicolls, 110.
Norman, 39. 56, 109, 146.
Norris, 152. 170.
Nourse, 4, 15, 29, 121.
Nowell, 59.
Nurse, 101, 143.

Oakes, 96, 97.
Oakman, 147.
Obear, 148, 160.
Ober, 77.
O'Brian, 143.
O'Brien, 108.
O'Conner, 147, 157, 161.
Odell, 11. 12, 20, 28, 37, 56.
Odlin, 154.
Oliver, 60, 133.
Orne, 24, 25, 40, 77, 124, 159.
Osgood, 49, 148, 154, 160.
Ostrum, 152.

Palfray, 133, 159, 163, 164.
Palfrey, 4, 21, 36, 45. 48, 56, 68, 71, 75, 90, 97, 105, 116, 124, 128. 132.
Parker, 17, 44, 96, 102, 131.
Parnel, 136.
Parrotte, 2.
Parsons. 10, 15, 47.
Pascal, 97, 101, 111.
Paterson, 72, 102.
Patfield. 170.
Patten, 31, 73, 74, 81, 92, 127, 153.
Patterson. 1. 2, 19, 20, 48, 73, 77, 79. 90, 91. 97, 98, 105, 107, 109, 115, 127, 131, 139, 152, 156, 161, 162.
Peabody, 67, 93, 131, 149.
Peach, 106, 130.
Peale, 101.
Peck, 129.
Peele, 21, 22, 23, 35, 64, 79, 80, 85, 88, 104, 115, 151, 162, 165.
Peirce, 3, 4.
Perkins, 25, 27. 30. 51, 60, 70, 71, 74, 86, 99, 117, 136, 151, 157.
Perry, 169, 170.
Perveare, 156.
Peters, 56, 109, 146, 164.
Phelps, 120, 136.
Philips. 93, 113.
Phillips, 25, 43, 54, 58.
Philpot, 95, 111.
Phippen. 2, 9, 16, 17. 19, 21, 32, 36. 37. 38, 39, 49, 51, 59, 60, 63, 70, 71, 79, 81, 97, 108, 110, 119, 122, 123, 129, 138, 142.
Pickering, 38, 90, 91, 119, 130.
Picket, 79, 110.
Pickman, 7, 46, 130, 140, 141.
Pierce, 61, 105, 130, 147, 153, 159.
Pitman, 38.
Plantine, 141.
Poole, 109, 120, 138.

Porter, 60, 61, 88, 89, 124, 163, 165.
Potter, 65, 112.
Prat, 1, 81.
Preston, 6, 21, 44, 52, 69, 70, 117, 148, 150.
Price, 108.
Prince, 11, 42, 75, 81, 82, 105, 116, 142, 152, 153, 156.
Proctor, 108.
Pulcifer. 166.
Punchard; 123.
Putnam, 10, 17, 57, 58, 73, 165.

Raftlin, 103.
Ramsdall, 113.
Ramsdell. 135.
Randall, 80, 112, 135.
Rankin, 79.
Rantoul, 69, 117, 148, 149.
Ratchliffe, 46.
Read, 142, 156.
Reath, 65.
Reed, 35. 50, 123.
Reeves, 106.
Reinar, 34.
Renew, 1.
Renough. 39.
Rhue, 26, 91, 106. 107, 116, 138, 147, 161, 170.
Rhuee. 121.
Rice, 75, 98, 163.
Richards, 122.
Richardson, 7, 27, 28, 30, 36. 48, 51, 67. 73, 80, 87, 101, 125, 129. 130, 132, 136, 146, 160.
Ridgway, 140.
Rind. 74.
Roach, 5.
Robbins, 145.
Robinson, 134, 155.
Rochstein, 54.
Rogers, 25, 51, 76, 125, 155, 156.
Romiere, 41.
Ropes, 3, 16, 29, 30, 39, 48, 50, 53, 60, 86, 95, 100, 105, 131, 134, 162, 165.
Ross. 110.
Rowell, 114, 139, 148, 150.
Rue, 53. 75.
Ruee, 32, 64.
Ruewing, 111.
Rust, 160, 165.
Ryan, 121.

Sabteh, 149.
Sage, 24, 26, 27, 68, 69, 71, 81. 108, 156.
Saunders, 16, 93, 165.
Sauward, 151.
Sayward, 127.
Schetswell, 148.
Searle. 8. 34, 45, 50, 52, 89, 101, 141.
Sennert, 46.
Servi, 128.
Servy, 37.
Shad, 34, 35, 69.
Shatswell, 114.

Shaw, 153.
Shed, 71.
Shehane, 13, 14, 21, 45, 62, 72, 90, 99, 125.
Shelden, 74.
Sheldon, 81, 133.
Shelton, 116.
Sibly, 59, 61.
Silsbee, 8, 14, 19, 20, 22, 34, 35, 37, 41, 47, 69, 77, 78, 79, 81, 82, 92, 98, 108, 121, 129, 131, 137, 141, 142, 152, 153, 156.
Silsbey, 110.
Silver, 2, 5, 84, 97, 101, 102, 111, 112.
Sinclair, 16, 69.
Skerry, 138, 139, 146, 164.
Skinner, 126.
Slade, 66.
Slate, 34, 86.
Sleuman, 5. 168.
Sloacum, 25, 161.
Sloaly, 38.
Slocum, 55.
Smith, 11, 13. 24. 25, 27, 30, 31, 32, 43, 47, 49, 58, 62, 68, 71, 72, 76, 78, 83, 87, 94, 95, 97, 99, 101, 106, 111, 121, 129, 131, 139. 165, 167.
Southward, 111, 136, 162.
Sparrow, 40.
Squires, 23, 49.
Standon, 151.
Stanley, 62, 76, 77, 79.
Stearns, 160, 170.
Stephens, 26, 39, 53, 57.
Sterling, 108.
Stevely, 65.
Stevens, 9, 55. 66, 87, 112.
Steward, 42, 43.
Stickney, 59, 91, 157.
Stileman, 21, 66, 99.
Stillman, 57.
Stivers, 168.
Stocker, 9, 48, 70.
Stoddard, 64.
Stoddart, 102, 149.
Stone, 26, 36, 42, 74, 90, 99, 131, 139, 144, 154, 164.
Street, 72, 106.
Strout, 10, 52, 57, 80.
Sullivan, 34, 147.
Swaney, 120.
Swasey, 20, 31, 32, 34, 36, 37, 54, 65, 96, 97, 100, 107, 117, 119, 125, 146, 147.
Sweetzer, 67.
Swett, 82, 107, 132.
Symmes, 20, 100.
Symonds, 15, 30, 136, 139.
Syms, 31.

Talbot, 143.
Tannenhall, 124.
Tapley, 111.
Tarbox, 62, 77.
Taylor, 23, 25, 49.
Tazell, 84.
Teague, 138.
Telbert, 18.
Thayer, 46.

INDEX OF NAMES.

Thomas, 22, 29, 98, 99, 137, 138.
Thompson, 30, 47.
Thresher. 127.
Tibbets, 82, 83.
Timothy, 151.
Titcombe, 48.
Tousel, 72.
Townsend, 3, 5. 23, 33, 39, 55, 60, 64, 66, 67, 73, 82, 88, 90, 104, 125, 141.
Tozer, 116.
Tozzer, 1, 41, 54, 77, 118, 127. 131, 145, 152.
Trask, 72, 163, 165, 166.
Traske, 60.
Tripp, 131.
Trow, 55.
Tucker, 112.
Tufts, 64.
Turner, 42, 122.
Twiss, 69.
Twisse. 72, 103.
Tyler, 31.
Tytler, 81, 116.

Ulmar, 82.
Ulmer, 35, 84, 85, 112.
Underwood, 73.
Upton, 129, 134, 141.

Vaicou, 39.
Valpey, 49, 87.
Valpy, 18, 38, 39, 40, 50, 54, 59, 77, 103, 146.
Vanderfort, 127.
Very, 35, 37.
Victory, 74, 121.
Vikery, 107.
Vincent, 18, 19, 26, 47, 48, 56, 59, 118, 130, 169.

Vincents, 47.

Wait, 168.
Walden, 63, 74.
Walker, 31.
Wallace, 133.
Ward, 7, 8, 15, 28, 29, 38, 54, 62, 68. 69, 71, 99. 105, 112, 118, 120, 123, 133, 136, 137, 141, 149, 153, 155, 158.
Wardilloe, 29.
Warner, 61. ·
Waters, 8, 21, 24, 26, 37, 38, 45, 69, 72, 77, 78, 95, 110, 122, 127, 152, 163, 169.
Watson. 1, 2, 10, 38, 96, 102, 115, 119, 130.
Watts, 130.
Webb, 7, 9, 10, 15, 18, 22, 23, 26, 29, 31, 32, 33, 36. 43, 44, 47, 50, 56, 57, 58, 60, 61, 62, 66, 73, 74, 75, 76, 77, 80, 81, 84, 85, 86, 87, 92, 95, 96, 99, 105, 107, 108, 115. 118, 120, 124, 126, 127, 128, 130, 133, 135, 143, 156.
Wedger, 125, 132.
Welcome, 21, 31, 68, 88, 121, 123, 143, 146, 163.
Welden, 67.
Wellman, 9, 15, 19, 46, 53, 56, 57.
Wells, 138, 143.
Welman, 4, 53, 75, 82, 84, 87, 98. 112, 116, 117, 118, 136, 154, 160, 163, 168.
Welsh, 34.
Wendell, 37.
West, 84.
Western, 80.
Weston, 87, 125.

Wheatland, 54.
Whipple, 167.
White, 8, 14, 16, 18, 36, 43, 52, 59, 65, 66, 80. 87, 90, 96, 124, 135, 144, 162, 164.
Whitefoot, 12, 31, 51, 64, 77, 115, 145, 149.
Whitehead, 23.
Whitford, 24, 46, 60, 85, 86, 116, 132, 133, 139.
Whittemore, 3, 10, 18, 57, 65, 77, 144, 146, 150, 155, 160.
Whitwell, 159.
Widger, 46, 62.
Wiederberg, 17.
Wiley, 121.
Williams. 14, 17. 20. 31, 32, 61, 68, 74, 82, 98, 100, 106, 107, 115, 119, 121, 124, 132, 161, 165.
Willick, 145.
Willis, 4, 34.
Wills, 81.
Winchester, 63.
Wing, 93.
Winn, 168.
Woodberry. 144.
Woodhull, 154.
Woodkind, 13, 45.
Woodman, 54, 83, 147.
Woods, 75.
Wormstead, 34.
Wright, 129, 141.
Wyatt, 24, 25, 32, 33, 34, 47, 116, 117, 154.
Wyatts, 11.
Wyman, 46.

Yell, 160.
Young, 110, 141.

www.ingramcontent.com/pod-product-compliance
Lightning Source LLC
Chambersburg PA
CBHW052059230426
43662CB00036B/1705